Relaciones

AN ACCOUNT of things seen and learned by Father Jerónimo de Zárate Salmerón from the Year 1538 to Year 1626. This is the first English translation to appear in book form. Purported to have been written about 1626 or 1627. The translation is by

ALICIA RONSTADT MILICH

and the foreword by
Dr. DONALD C. CUTTER

JEMEZ MISSION
Monument to Zárate Salmerón,
the principal builder of the church

...ciones

By ZARATE SALMERON

286139

HORN & WALLACE *Publishers*

HORN & WALLACE PUBLISHERS, INC., Box 4204
Albuquerque, New Mexico

Contents

Foreword

The history of any area depends in great measure on the quantity of documentation that is available to the researcher, to the student, and to the casual reader. Though in some circles it seems the vogue to exalt the synthesizer of materials, it is precisely among these interpretive historians that the basic documents are most appreciated, for the original manuscripts are the life blood of the narrative of history. In New Mexico we are indeed fortunate in having many fine basic documents for study; but no area is ever possessed of enough of these building blocks of history. Frequently it is the high points of history, the great expeditions, the struggling period of the first few years of precarious colonial existence, or the great cataclysms such as the Pueblo Revolt of 1680 in New Mexico that are the subjects of lengthy contemporary accounts. This is as it should be. But the history of an area takes on additional dimension when accounts are available which deal with some of the less startling and impressive episodes. It is even more worthwhile when a lengthy document possesses elements of both of these values. Such dual value is found in the reading of the *Relaciones* of Franciscan Father Gerónimo de Zárate Salmerón. This account contains what historians might classify as secondary descriptions of many of the events which preceded Spain's occupation of the northward salient called New Mexico. These secondary accounts, written not many years after the events being described, have the great advantage of reflecting almost contemporary opinion of such activities as the explorations of Fray Marcos de Niza and of Francisco Vásquez de Coronado, and the occupation of New Mexico under the leadership of Juan de Oñate. The Zárate Salmerón narration also reflects the still prevailing opinion that the great treasures to be found amidst the Northern Mystery of the North American interior were still anticipated. Even the imaginary geography including such items as Quivira and the Strait of Anian was not as yet dispelled, and the writing continually reflects the expectation of great things to be encountered.

The Zárate Salmerón account of New Mexico and the northern frontier is not the introspective work of a humble, discalced Franciscan in a far off province chronicling the prosaic events of a distant mission field; it is the clarion call of the missionary stimulating the Spanish crown through the beating of drums and the blowing of trumpets. Appealing at once to the cupidity of the Spanish Monarchy and its ever-present and insatiable need for money, and to the great Papal surrogation of power in the Royal Patronage which made the Crown responsible for conversion of the infidel, the account alternately stimulates the acquisitive tendencies of the Spaniard and challenges his conscience to obey the Great Command of spreading the Gospel of Catholic Christianity to every living creature. At times the literate Franciscan becomes carried away by his somewhat fanciful and occasionally prophetic descriptions of the wealth in mines to be uncovered in the northern area of New Spain, as the kingdom of Mexico was then called. Alternately Zárate Salmerón seems to be appropriately preoccupied with the welfare of such a great harvest of souls which lacked only the laborers to bring them into the fold.

Within New Mexico Zárate Salmerón was resident from 1621 until 1626. It is surprising that he was able to accomplish so much, for he is credited with building a convent and a temple, of baptizing over 6,500 of his Jemez Indian parishioners, and of writing a *Doctrine* in the language of his converts, indicating a linguistic facility not always demonstrated by frontier missionaries and one which must have cost many hours of study to obtain. A strong spiritual zeal for expansion of the conversions of New Mexico motivated the greatest of this Mexican-born friar's achievements, or at least the one for which he has won a place in the area's history—the compilation of his invaluable *Relaciones*. In its primary purpose this account did not result in the great awakening of interest that Zárate Salmerón had hoped. It is impossible to know at this late date what side effects his account might have had upon governmental officials, fellow Franciscans, or upon the crown. It did certainly paint the area in the brilliant tones of later day publicists, for to the 17th Century priest the province was truly a Land of Enchantment. In his concern for New Mexico and its native inhabitants, Fray Gerónimo has left us an early key to the understanding of regional history.

As a result of his methodology in his presentation of information, Zárate Salmerón's account is not restricted to a mere recitation of contemporary problems of New Mexico, though he did at times comment incisively upon these. As a calculated stimulus to positive action to be taken by the Spanish crown for the purpose of assuring the future of New Mexico, the devout Franciscan priest brought to bear on his topic any information which might lead to that end, however speculative and remote the material. As a result, he was interested in an area extending from the coasts of Upper and Lower California to Newfoundland and beyond, but always for the purpose of demonstrating the relationship of those areas to the projected larger Spanish interest in the place of his missionary activity in the several pueblos where he served in New Mexico.

Many years after preparation of the original *Relaciones,* a response to Zárate Salmerón's comments was written as *Apuntamientos que sobre el terreno hizo el Padre Juan Amando Niel de la Compañía de Jesús y pueden servir de esplicacion á las Memorias que del Nuevo-México y partes articas de la América Septentrional, nos dejó manuscritas el Padre Jerónimo de Zárate Salmerón, Predicador de los Menores de la Provincia del Santo Evangelio Méxicana: Motivos de escribir estos apuntamientos,* a lengthy and interesting document in imitation of the Franciscan's efforts, but intended as a corrective to the overstatements of the earlier work. Purportedly written by a Jesuit priest, Father Juan Amando Niel, these *Apuntamientos* have been branded as a forgery by a leading Jesuit historian, Father Ernest J. Burrus, at least insofar as there never existed on the northern frontier of New Spain any priest by that name. The Niel account gives evidence of being the work of a literate military officer or some government official, and seems to possess as a theme the desire to discredit Father Zárate Salmerón. This Niel polemic is another subject, and one of only marginal concern here. It is significant, however, that neither the Zárate Salmerón nor the Niel has been published in book form in English, though both have appeared in Spanish several times in documentary collections.

Niel's *Apuntamientos,* despite its purposes, not only bears a very close resemblance to the Zárate Salmerón *Relaciones,* but by statistical analysis the former work is made up of 39.3 per cent direct transcription from the latter. Much of the remainder is a discussion of minor points based on the hindsight of Niel having written three quarters of a century later. Principally the Niel voices the lament of every historical researcher in asking why the ancient writer did not take the trouble to supply just a few more details concerning those things in which the more modern writer was interested.

A perusal of the Spanish original of the Zárate Salmerón account reveals the difficulty to be encountered in attempting an English language version. At best translation is a difficult historical art, and this when the original is unencumbered by regionalisms and special vocabulary. When the ecclesiastical language of the early 17th Century is compounded with now long outdated Hispanic grammar and punctuation, the job becomes complicated. Fortunately for the clarity and meaning of Alicia Ronstadt Milich's present translation, the translator brings to her work a veritable lifetime of experience with Spanish, both classical and modern. Born in a bilingual Arizona family along the international border, and resident for some 15 years in Madrid, the translator has also taught Spanish for many years in the high schools and universities of California. She is one of the truly bilingual people who suffers no disability in either language. A lifelong interest in the Spanish Borderlands and a Master of Arts degree with a thesis topic in Southwestern History have added to Alicia Milich's competence; but it has been in the crucible of work with the document and in the field that the translator's mettle has been tested. The result is most satisfying. A faithful and readable translation, reduced from typically Spanish sentences of the original which are as lengthy as they are confusing, the product presented in this work preserves the flavor of the original. As always, to do this results in some compromise, with Father Zárate Salmerón becoming the beneficiary of some of his most confusing sentences possessing greater clarity because of the discernment of the modern translator. When the ancient idiom of the original is beyond recovery, Alicia Milich has not hesitated to admit this and to permit the reader to exercise what little light he might add. The present translation has been carefully done to preserve as much as possible the spelling, accentuation, and unique expression of Zárate Salmerón's original *Relaciones*. Some inconsistencies of spelling and particularly of accentuation have resulted from these efforts.

Hubert Howe Bancroft, the great collector and compiler of Western North Americana, considers the Zárate Salmerón account as a prime source. In his highly laudatory evaluation of the *Relaciones,* Bancroft points out that the Franciscan was more concerned with the activities of the past and of the future than he was with the present in which he lived. Doubtless this has deprived us of his fully calculated judgment concerning certain facets of early 17th Century New Mexico history; but it has added greatly to our knowledge of the various subjects upon which the devout padre had a veritable fixation—the Indians, their conversion, and the permanent and profitable exploitation of the northern frontier area. A recent historian of the period, Jack D. Forbes, places the priestly account as about our only source of knowledge concerning a portion of this period. Others have held it in high regard. Used by historians and anthropologists in its Spanish original, it is surprising that up to now this valuable document has not been published in English as a book. It is this long-standing oversight on the part of historians that has motivated the translation and annotation that Alicia Milich has brought forth and which is herein presented.

Donald C. Cutter
The University of New Mexico

Introduction

New Mexico has been particularly fortunate in having chronicles and chroniclers of its early history. The relative literacy of the many Franciscans who served in the area has been in large measure responsible for an interesting contemporary record. One of these early literate figures was Fray Gerónimo de Zárate Salmerón, whose account of New Mexico and associated areas is a reflection of his interest in the conversion to Christianity of the natives.

Although it was generally believed that Fray Gerónimo de Zárate Salmerón entered New Mexico in 1618, his name appears on the list of the six friars who went north to New Mexico with the supply caravan of 1621.[1] According to most accounts he entered there in 1618. The Benavides Memorial, another early account, states that Zárate Salmerón went to Jemez at that time, where he converted the Indians, that he was a good minister and linguist, and that he founded at the principal pueblo a very beautiful convent and a magnificent temple dedicated to Saint Joseph. In Fray Zárate Salmerón's own words in the *Relaciones,* he sacrificed himself to the Lord among the pagans,—toiling chiefly among the Jemez, of whom he baptized 6,566 and in whose language he wrote a *Doctrina,* or theological treatise. Above all Zárate Salmerón was eager to convert new tribes and it was with a view to overcome obstacles in this direction that in 1626 he went to Mexico, bringing with him the *Relaciones*.

This most important chronicle has two central themes, the first to stimulate missionary activity, the second to impress the king with the potential riches of the northern area of New Spain. The second theme doubtless was in support of the first. New Mexico, "el otro México," was a vast region extending into limitless areas with no definite boundaries, its potential for development beyond the imagination of that time.

The period prior to Zárate Salmerón's stay in New Mexico had been one filled with great troubles between Church and State. Ill feeling had grown to a stage of violence and there seemed to be no way of coming to any agreement. According to the law of that time the authority of the state was to predominate. This, however, did not work out in practice, the Church having supreme power. The two basic causes of misunderstanding were: 1.) the problem of ecclesiastical jurisdiction and authority; and 2.) the problem of Indian relations. The laws and courts of the Church were to be upheld and respected. Despite all this trouble between Franciscans and government, the mission program continued to advance, and the caravans with provisions and men for the missions arrived regularly.[2]

When Zárate Salmerón arrived in New Mexico affairs in that remote region had reached such a troubled state that in Mexico the government was considering whether the northern area was worth colonizing. It was believed to be a poor area, its minerals and other potential wealth being unknown. Nevertheless, the Franciscans had won their appeal to carry on their apostolic work, for their zeal to bring souls into the faith was a sincere motive.

The area of "el otro México" reflected in some measure the general trend of conditions throughout the Indies. However, because of the relative simplicity of political, social, and economic conditions, and the isolation of this area, Santa Fe being 1,500 miles from Mexico City, every issue assumed greater importance than would have been the case if life there had been more complex and varied. Relations became intensely personal, prejudiced, and violent in this milieu.

According to the Benavides Memorial, (p. 251), Fray Zárate Salmerón was the first resident missionary in the Jemez pueblos. These pueblos were situated southwest of Santa Fe among very rugged mountains which were rich in deposits of silver and copper. After the main pueblo burned down, it was abandoned and the Indians went to other regions.

The New Mexico mission area extended from Pecos on the east to Taos on the north, then to the Jemez pueblos to the northwest. These villages were on the frontier between the main pueblo area and the Navajo country. The Jemez nation was one of the most belligerent of the area and rose in revolt in 1623. It was not subdued. Navajo raids and famine weakened it in the following years. It was not until the period of Benavides, 1625-1629, that mission activities were resumed in the Jemez area. Zárate Salmerón also served at Zia and Sandia among the Queres. Alone he pacified and converted the pueblo of Acoma after a revolt.

The Padre was delighted with the New Mexico country, its climate, people, products, agriculture, and minerals, but was displeased with the lethargy of the Spaniards, who were not fond of working. In spite of the utmost perils and difficulties, he built churches and monasteries, and he wrote a valuable document.

In the *Relaciones* the Navajos are mentioned for the first time. Zárate Salmerón calls them Apaches de Nabaju. Reference is made also by Zárate Salmerón to six Zuni pueblos through which Oñate passed on his way to the Gulf of California. The Franciscan writes about the very high quality garnets found in New Mexico at Picuries, and about the mineral deposits in the Socorro Mountains and of the extent of mineral wealth of the province in general.

Contradictory opinions regarding Zárate Salmerón's account exist. However, although it is considered to be inaccurate in a few details, it is indeed a valuable document, and a most important source of information on New Mexico. Besides containing information not obtainable elsewhere on the ethnography of western Arizona and eastern California, it includes data on the Rio Grande pueblos and on that of Jemez that are of permanent value.

Due to the fact that Zárate Salmerón wrote the *Relaciones* after his return to Mexico, a few details may be in error. According to France V. Scholes, Zárate Salmerón's account of the deaths of Father López and Father Rodríguez by Indians of Puaray in 1582 "is replete with error."[3] Zárate Salmerón was not an eyewitness to all the events, obtaining some of his information from persons who had been on the scene, and from original documents that are now lost. Regarding his account of the Oñate expedition, Zárate Salmerón probably obtained his information from Fray Francisco de Escobar, who accompanied the expedition and whose own account may be found in the Archive of the Indies in Sevilla. Despite occasional errors and the secondary nature of some of his information, valuable historical data are found only in Zárate Salmerón's *Relaciones*. For example, this is seen in a quotation from the Benavides Memorial: "No other evidence has been found that Perea served in New Mexico prior to 1629 —than Salmerón's account—that Perea[4] was commissary in 1614, succeeding Fray Alonso Peinado, or 30 years after the death of Fray Juan Francisco López in 1581, and that he reinterred the bones of the latter in Sandia." One historian considers Zárate Salmerón to be our chief source of information on New Mexico from 1621 to 1626.[5] Hubert Howe Bancroft states that it is a very interesting and complete resume, the best extant,—being by no means confined to New Mexico and that the writer is "fully imbued with the spirit of his time."[6] That his *Relaciones* has caused argument among scholars is one more proof of its importance. One manuscript written in Mexico after 1730, a criticism of the alleged miracles of the mystic, María Jesús de Agreda, the Woman in Blue, states that Zárate Salmerón did not mention that large body of new Christians supposed to have been discovered in 1622. However, he does mention this fact in Chapter 136 of the *Relaciones*.

New documentary material was found by France V. Scholes in Spain and Mexico in 1927-28 concerning missions in New Mexico during the 17th Century. These documents contained descriptions and statistics of the individual missions with their churches, *conventos* and *visitas* and the numbers of Indians belonging to each mission. "It is a list which seems to have been part of, or supplementary to, the *Relaciones*. The edition of the *Relaciones* which is printed in the *Documentos para la Historia de México,* third series, does not contain such a list so that the *Relaciones* as we have had it is not complete." Salmerón's list contains more definite and more complete information than Benavides.[7]

Seventy years after Zárate Salmerón published his *Relaciones,* the Franciscan Fray Agustín de Vetancurt published an account called *Teatro Méxicano.* The third and fourth parts of this work, the *Crónica de la Provincia del Santo Evangelio de México* and the *Menologio Franciscano* contain important information concerning the Rio Grande Pueblos and New Mexico in general. These parts contain clear descriptions of the missions and the Indian villages along with population data previous to the Pueblo Revolt. In this respect, Vetancurt's work is considered an improvement upon Benavides, his approximate census approaching Zárate Salmerón's figures given 70 years before.

The *Relaciones* could not have been written earlier than 1627 since it was addressed to Franciscan Commissary General Fray Francisco de Apodaca,[8] who did not assume the post until that year.

There are several known copies of Zárate Salmerón's *Relaciones;* a copy of the *Relaciones* made by Fray Francisco García Figueroa and dated November 9th, 1792, is in the Real Academia de la Historia in Madrid, Spain. A second of this 1792 version is in the Archivo del Ministerio de Hacienda in Madrid, while the Archivo General de la Nación in Mexico has a third copy of the 1792 document.[9]

In 1856 the *Relaciones* was printed in a large edition, along with other works. This work was entitled *Documentos para la historia de México,* Tercera Serie, Imprenta de Vicente García Torres, México, Tomo Primero. This copy is faulty in several places. Hitherto there has been an English translation of the *Relaciones* by Charles F. Lummis in the magazine *Land of Sunshine,* in serial from June 1899 to May 1900.

Another edition of the *Relaciones* was published in Mexico by Vargas Rea, in 1949. This edition, however, contains only the chapters of the *Relaciones* which pertain to New Mexico.

Basically the present translation was made from *Documentos para servir a la Historia del Nuevo México 1538-1778,* Colección Chimalistac, Ediciones José Porrúa Turanzas, Madrid, 1962. Other versions have been consulted for comparison. This new edition has been done with the hope that it may serve to bring Zárate Salmerón's account to many who because of the difficulty of obtaining it, have not been able to use its wealth of knowledge.

Data concerning Fray Gerónimo de Zárate Salmerón are not ideally informative. There are many things that we would like to know about his life but we are required in large measure to depend on what he has said about himself and what can be gleaned from the fugitive references that we have in the documentary sources.

According to the Rosa Figueroa documents, Fray Gerónimo de Zárate Salmerón completed his novitiate and was professed in Mexico on October 6th, 1579 at the Convento Grande of Mexico City. He was a criollo, being born in Rio Alvarado, Mexico. This fact is significant.

José Mariano Beristáin de Souza in his *Biblioteca Hispano-Americana Septentrional* mentions that Fray Zárate Salmerón was a student of the Franciscan Province of the Santo Evangelio of Mexico and that he wrote other accounts.

Most of all one is impressed throughout these *Relaciones* with the zeal and piety of Fray Zárate Salmerón imbued with the spirit of his time to bring souls into the fold of Christianity. His great simplicity and understanding of humanity also reveal that he had a sense of humor along with a practical approach to greater things accomplished. There is no doubt that in the future scholars will find many more interesting and significant facts about him.

And now before closing this introduction I must add a few words of acknowledgement. I was particularly pleased to be asked to translate and edit these *Relaciones* of Zárate Salmerón, and I have had a very personal feeling about it as one whose family has long been here in the Southwest on both sides of the border. Father was born in Sonora and his stories of early days have left a deep impression on me. Through marriage Spain became my home for many years, after which I was to teach Spanish at the University of California at Los Angeles and in the high schools of Beverly Hills and Los Angeles. This past year spent here in New Mexico has been a particularly happy one and I have become steeped in its history, reading extensively and visiting many of the places in the *Relaciones*. I have tried to keep the spirit of the original along with the truth of its translation, hoping that it will be of value to many who hitherto have been unable to obtain it. Many wonderful friends have also helped to make this work a reality.

In addition, I wish to express my appreciation and thanks to Miss Eleanor Adams, to Dr. France V. Scholes, and to all the staff at the University of New Mexico Library who have been very kind in assisting me with information of documents and books. Above all I thank Dr. Donald C. Cutter, friend and teacher at the University of New Mexico, who has helped me so generously, guiding me, reading the manuscript, and assisting with innumerable details. I deeply appreciate his enthusiastic aid and encouragement without which this book might not have been written.

ALICIA RONSTADT MILICH

RELACIONES

DE TODAS LAS COSAS

QUE EN EL NUEVO-MEXICO SE HAN VISTO Y SABIDO,

ASI POR MAR COMO POR TIERRA,

DESDE EL AÑO DE 1538 HASTA EL DE 1626,

POR EL PADRE

GERONIMO DE ZARATE SALMERON,

predicador de la órden de los Menores de la provincia del Santo Evangelio.

DIRIGIDAS

A Nuestro Reverendisimo Padre Fray Francisco de Apodaca,

PADRE DE LA PROVINCIA DE CANTABRIA

y comisario general de todas las de esta Nueva-España.

ACCOUNT OF ALL THE THINGS THAT HAVE BEEN SEEN AND LEARNED IN NEW MEXICO BY SEA AS WELL AS BY LAND FROM THE YEAR 1538 UNTIL THE YEAR 1626

By

FATHER GERONIMO DE ZARATE SALMERON

Preacher of the Order of Minors
of the Province of the Holy Gospel.

To Our Most Reverend Father Fray Francisco de Apodaca, Father of the Province of Cantabria and Commissary General of all the Provinces of this New Spain.

Translated By
ALICIA RONSTADT MILICH

From: DOCUMENTOS PARA SERVIR A LA HISTORIA DEL NUEVO MÉXICO, 1538-1778.

Collección Chimalistac, 1962

Ediciones José Porrúa Turanzas,
Madrid.

Chapter 1

Approval

By order of our Most Reverend Fray Francisco de Apodaca,[10] commissary general of all the provinces and "custodias" of this New Spain, Florida, the Philippines, and New Mexico, I saw the accounts that Fray Gerónimo de Zárate Salmerón, preacher religious and son of this province of the Holy Gospel of the Order of Our Father Saint Francis, as a person who spent many years in those conversions and conquests, has gathered and compiled concerning the extensive provinces of New Mexico, and also what he saw and understood by his own labor and his work. And there being nothing in these accounts that is contrary to Our Holy Catholic Faith, rather there being more that would broaden it and spread it in those regions so filled with people as well as lacking in preachers and ministers to make it known, as I saw the situation and experienced it during the time I was there, I find it fitting and necessary for this purpose that these accounts be printed for the honor and glory of God, our Lord, and for the service of our Catholic King, Phillip. And in order that, seen in brief what others have written at greater length, it may be read by all, so that, the grandeur and richness of those kingdoms being known, there may be someone who will be moved to want to take charge of their conquest, and that many servants of our Lord who have offered themselves to the spiritual life of those souls so in need and who upon opening this door may enter through it, to preach the Holy Gospel. Having faith in this, and believing the truths contained therein and in the zeal of this religious, I feel that this account is very useful and worthwhile, that its author being a serious religious has taken very special care only to serve our Lord, and to win those souls. Thus I sign it with my name in this convent of San Francisco in Mexico, the 18th of August of this year of 1629. Fray Francisco de Velasco.[11]

Most Reverend Father:—Considering the invincible spirit and great desire that the religious of our seraphic religion have had and always have for the good of souls, preaching the Holy Gospel, carrying always in their hearts the words that Christ our Lord said to his disciples when he sent them to preach throughout the world; *predicate evangelium omni creature.*[12] With this fervent spirit we see that there is no corner nor remote place, where the religious of our father, Saint Francis, have not entered, and that in all the discoveries, they are the light that guides, whom all the rest follow, not even fearing to leave their lives in the hands of tyrants, accompanied by Christian counsel, our teacher. *Nolite timere eos qui occident corpus, animan autem nom pasunt occidere.*[13] And so they are the first ones who shed their blood preaching the Holy Gospel among the infidels. And I, insignificant and unworthy, the worst person in the world, wishing to finish my days among the heathens, preaching the word of God, for about eight years sacrificed myself to the Lord among the heathens of New Mexico. And having learned there the language of the Hemex[14] Indians, where I composed the Christian Doctrine, and prepared all the other important things for the ministry, in order to administer the Holy Sacraments among those natives, and having baptized in that nation 6,566 souls, without counting the many that I baptized in the pueblo of Cia,[15] and Santa Ana, of the Queres nation, I alone conquered and pacified El Peñol de Acoma that sustained a war with the Spaniards, building churches and convents along with other things that merit remembering, as are evident by accounts. However, I wanted to look for souls again to give to God, knowing about the innumerable ones that the inland has. From the north to the northeast and to the northwest, which is to both sides of due north, God has created these souls, whose enemy is the infernal dragon Satan. Having endeavored to enter there alone and without an escort, and my good intentions being unsuccessful, I determined to come here so that your Reverence may be informed of all those things concerning it, that he may take the means that are appropriate for the service of God our Lord whom one desires to serve and please.

And so that it may come to the attention of all the Spaniards, that God has in His keeping, so that these things may be enjoyed by whoever may help himself, which things stir worldly hearts more than they affect the improvement of souls, and by means of those interests the Spaniards ought to inhabit that new world, from which will result great temporal and spiritual advantages, I make known telling about each thing and where it is, such as gold, silver, pearls, coral, garnets, copper, lead, alum, sulphur, vitriol, magnate stone, and turquoise, the terrain and days' marches, and in which direction they ought to travel, and that with this account in their hands, it may serve as a compass and chart to those who may enter there, and that Your Reverence knowing these things, may with your Christianity, open the doors and give permission to those religious of ardor who may want to enter apostolically to shed their blood among those infidels. May laborers enter the vineyard of the Lord, for here there are too many, and there, there is no one to give bread to them, from which we can labor with very great conscientiousness. *Parbulli petierunt panen, et non erat qui frageret eis.*[16] And this expedition, apostolically without wages or any cost to His Majesty, and without soldiers, because if they are not such as they should be, it is better to go alone than in bad company, trusting in Divine Favor and not in human strength, and this, if I am not deceiving myself, God ordered Zechariah to tell Zerubbabel: *non in exercitu, nec in robore, sed in spiritu meo.*[17] This is the surest way. *Rogate ergo dominum messis ut mitat operarios in messem suam.*[18] I know well that many religious fast and perform penances with great effort, asking God to open the door to the great harvest of converts that exist there, burning in the fire of divine love and fervor for the good of souls, as true sons of my father, Saint Francis, desiring to enter there, trusting that God will not fail them in their greatest trial and necessity. For it is His word speaking with the just man who is in trouble: *Cum ipso sum in Tribulatione.*[19] And it is not right, Most Reverend Father, that because of our negligence and laziness those souls should lack so much good. It is an apostolic undertaking, and as I know that Your Reverence, in promoting and supporting this cause with your very pious heart, it will be carried out as it should, I have taken on this work. May Your Reverence receive it as from a humble younger son who in everything wishes to do right and that the word of God may continue spreading through those remote places of that New World. May God protect Your Most Reverend Father.—Minor son. Fr. Gerónimo de Zárate Salmerón.

Chapter 2

The News Begins
1538

I.

In the year 1538, when D. Antonio de Mendoza[1] was Viceroy of this New Spain,[2] four ships of the Marqués del Valle[3] sailed on a first attempt to discover the Californias and the coast of the South Sea.[4] And on those vessels went three religious who had been sent to the discovery by the holy Fray Antonio de Ciudad Rodrigo,[5] who was at that time provincial of this province of the Holy Gospel. They arrived at the entrance of the Californias at the port which is now called La Paz. It is in 24 degrees latitude and, as the land did not seem as good to them as they would have wanted, they returned.

II.

During the same year the Father Provincial sent two other religious[1] by land along the same coast of the South Sea, traveling northward through Jalisco and Nueva Galicia.[2] These two priests went along with a captain and 12 soldiers who were going in search of mines. After they crossed all the land that had been discovered and conquered in that area, they found two well-opened roads. The captain chose the one to the right, and he followed it saying that he was going to the north, and after journeying a few days they came upon such harsh land that he obliged them to turn back, which they did. One of the two religious became ill and he also turned back; and the other, with two Indian interpreters that he was taking with him, continued on the left-hand road toward the coast, a very straight road. He arrived at a land inhabited by poor Indians who came out to receive the priest believing him to be something from Heaven. They touched him and kissed his habit. More than 300 Indians accompanied him from day to day. Some of them would go off to hunt hares, rabbits, and deer, which are abundant all through that land. They first gave food to the priest so that he might eat, and the rest they divided among themselves. And so, in this way, he traveled more than 200 leagues. On almost all this route he received news of a land densely populated by people who wear clothes, who have terraced houses and not of a single story but of many. Other people, they said, were settled on the banks of a great river where there are many walled pueblos, and that they have wars with each other, and that after crossing that river, there were many other larger pueblos with much richer people, and that there were larger cows than ours and other animals not seen in Castile.

III.

Many important fleets by sea and armies by land had already left seeking this land, and God had concealed it from all of them and had revealed it to a poor, shabby, and humble friar of Saint Francis who discovered it and saw it before they did: *Quia abscondisti hec a sapientibus et prudentibus, et rebelasti ea parabulis.*[1] All I can say is: this religious returned to tell the news of what he had seen and learned; and, as soon as this news was spread, many Spaniards wanted to go there. The provincial, who at that time was Fray Marcos Denia,[2] to make sure of what that religious had said, went ahead before the Spaniards entered and he reached there in the shortest time that he could. He found the priest's account to be correct and he affirmed this truthfully as a man who had seen it.

IV.

The Viceroy D. Antonio de Mendoza offered to go himself in person on this journey in order to prevent the thefts and wicked deeds that soldiers commit on such occasions. But serious affairs prevented his going, and so, in his place, he sent Francisco Vásquez Coronado who took as his assistants the Father Provincial of this province and four other religious, true sons of our father Saint Francis.[1]

Chapter 3

Francisco Vásquez Coronado's Trip
to New Mexico

V.

Before Francisco Vásquez Coronado entered New Mexico, the Viceroy had sent a fleet to the Californias, with Francisco Alarcón[1] as fleet commander and Marcos Ruiz as field commander. This fleet was lost without accomplishing anything; these people returned here to New Spain; and as nothing came of it, I shall not spend any more time concerning this expedition.

VI.

Francisco Vásquez left this city of Mexico in the year 1540, and after crossing the provinces of Chametla, Culhuacan,[1] Sinaloa, they entered by way of the Valle de Corazones[2] and through the valleys of Sonora which are more than 60 leagues long. He reached the Province of Cuñi, and established his camp in the pueblo of Zíbola which is the head of that province.[3] From this place he sent 30 soldiers[4] to find the sea and to learn if the fleet appeared, which, according to the instructions it carried, they were to meet in so many degrees north latitude. These men continued traveling to the northwest and to the sea or gulf of California. In latitude 39 degrees[5] they found no trace of the fleet; all they found were two anchored ships, and awnings set up as tents belonging to some mulattoes resembling Morrillos[6] or Chinamen. Going up to them, they asked them by signs where they were from and what they were looking for; and they (the mulattoes), also by signs, said they came from very far away. Some understood that they were from Great China, others that they were from Asia Major, and that they were buying metals and amber that the Indians brought down from a mountain range that joins the sea. The soldiers returned to give an account of what

they had seen to Francisco Vásquez Coronado, but they did not find
him in Cuñi, for he had gone to explore the Zíbola plains with its
innumerable herds of animals of this name. He settled his camp
on these plains, and from here he sent 30 soldiers to find the great
city of Quivira.[7] They kept on traveling to the northwest and even
closer to the north than to the northwest. These soldiers say that
they arrived at a very highly populated city surrounded by a wall
and gates, and they did not enter it because they were so few. I do
not dare to state here the great riches of this city, although they have
told me about them in accounts. The truth is that these soldiers returned and wanted the entire army, which was 400 men, to go there.
They came to tell all this to their general, whom they found out
of his mind, caused by a fall from his horse. Others say that he was
pretending this because he had recently married when he started
this journey and that he loved his wife so much that he spent all his
time crying and sighing for her; and, although they begged him
earnestly to go and see what they had seen, he answered the same as
that other guest of whom Saint Luke tells us: *Uxorem duxi et ideo
nom posum ire.*[8] Finally he consoled everyone by saying that winter
was now beginning and that he wanted to go back to Mexico and
that he would return another year, but he did not return. Since
then everyone is so anxious that this expedition be carried out, that
if it were announced there would be so many soldiers joining it, with
arms and horses, at their own expense, that there would be enough
men, saving His Majesty these costs. The important thing is a captain
that is fit for such discoveries, a Christian and unselfish, zealous in
God's law, and wanting to enrich the royal treasury.

VII.

On this expedition, before arriving at the great city of Quivira,
the Indians came out on the way and told these 30 soldiers that about
10 days' journey from there, on the coast of the North Sea,[1] some
white men were settled. These men wore clothes and were bearded,

they had swords and arquebuses, and also ships. There were other clear signs suggesting that these men are the Hollanders of New France.[2] Since then we have seen and talked here to Indian men and women who have reached the settlement of these Hollanders and have been with them. None of the Spaniards of New Mexico fails to know this, because it was in my time.

VIII.

And Francisco Vásquez Coronado returned to this city of Mexico with the Father Provincial and two companions.[1] There remained behind, among those Indians of the plains of Zíbola, the Apostolic Friars Juan de Padilla and Juan de la Cruz. A Portuguese named Andrés del Campo and two Indian lay brothers[2] also remained. And Father Padilla found out from the Indians about the great cities that are to the north and that if they would travel three moons he would come to where there are innumerable souls. In these good spirits, he set out to see them, accompanied by the Portuguese and lay brothers, leaving Fray Juan de la Cruz alone. Having traveled some days, they came upon the sight of a great settlement of the Quivira and the Indians came out to meet them in battle. The religious seeing them come, understood their bad intentions and begged the Portuguese, who had his horse, to take flight and so, too, he entreated the lay brothers, who after all, being swift Indians, would follow him. Fray Juan de Padilla would wait for those bloodthirsty wolves to glut themselves on him, while the others fled. They did this, and, hiding on a hillock to watch, they saw how the saintly man waited for the Indians on his knees. They came and killed him. The same thing happened to the saintly Fray Juan de la Cruz, whom the Indians also killed at the place where he had remained. The Portuguese and the lay brothers escaped and, when they arrived here, they told what had happened; and it is something to think about, that there is no discovered corner in all this New Spain where the first colonizer is not a friar of Saint Francis. They are the first to have shed their blood in order that, with such good mortar, the edifice be lasting and eternal. Nothing was done about this for 40 years until 1581, when God willed to make it known through a lay priest of my father Saint Francis named Fray Agustín Ruiz,[3] who, while he was in the Valle de Santa Bárbara, which is 200 leagues from this city of Mexico, and who, while he was among those Concho Indians, learned that to the north there were great cities. He asked permission from the prelates to go among those infidels. They granted it and gave him two dedicated religious, exemplary young theologians, named Fray Francisco López, who went as commissary, and Fray Juan de Santa María. Then they were joined by 12 soldiers and a captain who were going in search of mines. They left Santa Bárbara traveling 200 leagues to the north and arrived at the province of the Indians of the Tiguas Nation. These Indians are settled on the banks of the Río del Norte,[4] 400 leagues from the city of Mexico. Arriving at the pueblo of Puaray they decided to turn back and so they did, for there were too many Indians there and not enough Spaniards. The religious remained there among the Indians, and knowing that all that region was densely populated by several nations, they went forth to see them all. When the three religious arrived among the Tanos Indians at their pueblo of Galisteo and saw their docility, they agreed that one of them should come here to Mexico to tell the prelates what they had seen, so that more religious might go to cultivate that vineyard. Fray Juan de Santa María, who was a great astronomer[5] offered himself to go on this journey, and, tracing out the land, he found, by his calculation, that he had traveled less and more directly, and so he left from behind the Puaray Mountains[6] in order to cross the salt beds, and from there to cut straight over to the ford of the Rio del Norte, 100 leagues this side of Mexico. But his good intent was not realized, for on the third day after he bade his brother companions farewell, he went to take a nap under a tree, and the Tiguas Indians, of the pueblo that is now called San Pablo, killed him and burned his bones. The other two priests returned to the pueblo of Puaray, where they had been before, enjoying good, friendly treatment. They stayed there with the Indians, learning their language, until the devil, being our enemy, played his tricks. One afternoon, while Fray Francisco López was praying, a little more than the range of an arquebus shot away from the pueblo, an Indian killed him with two blows of a war club[7] that struck him on the temples, as the marks on his skull show. And the Indians of that pueblo confess it, for there are still many Indians who witnessed his death, and they revealed the place where his body was buried. Fray Agustín Ruiz shrouded him and buried him according to our custom, inside the village. The captain of the pueblo showed signs of sorrow over the death of the religious, and in order that the same thing should not happen to the lay priest who was left behind, he took him with him to the pueblo called Santiago, a league and a half up the river. Here he guarded him as carefully as he could but, in an unmindful moment, the Indians came and did the same thing, killing Fray Agustín Ruiz also, and threw his body into the river which was at high water. And so these Tiguas Indians killed these three priests, and it has been declared that in that humble, remote place there are five martyrs for the honor and glory of God. This blood has also borne fruit to the land, for through it, there are 34,650 baptized souls. This number is taken from the baptismal records, and does not include the many souls that at this time are being converted. And with the greatest fervor, in this mystery, the laborers in the vineyard of Our Lord are working and have built 43 churches in all, large and small, at their own cost. All this has been done without our lord the King having spent one real,[8] saving His Majesty all these expenses, and as ministers keep going in with each expedition, this conversion is always spreading.

IX.

The soldiers who left that land when these three priests stayed

behind in the pueblo of Puaray notified the prelates of how they
had remained there and of the great danger that they were in.
While the Viceroy was planning to take measures in order to find
out about them, Antonio de Espejo, a very honest and devout man
of ours, offered himself to go on this journey.

X.

Antonio de Espejo entered New Mexico in the year 1538[1] during the month of July, taking with him a religious named Fray
Bernardino Beltrán, true son of our father, Saint Francis, and before
reaching New Mexico[2] they learned that the Indians had killed the
priests. When Antonio de Espejo and his soldiers arrived at the
pueblo of Puaray, the Indians, out of fear, abandoned the pueblo,
but they did not escape punishment for they paid dearly for it.

XI.

I shall not write about this journey of Antonio de Espejo, nor
Castaño's, nor of Captain Nemorcctc's expedition,[1] nor of Humaña,[2]
because they all saw the same thing, and so it is enough that it be told
once. The body of the holy Fray Juan López was hidden for more
than 33 years, at the end of which an Indian of the pueblo of
Puaray, an eye-witness of his death and burial, revealed it to Fray
Estévan de Perea,[3] who was commissary of those provinces and a
great minister among those natives. The body, or better said, the
bones, were carried with every reverence and respect by the priests
in funeral robes and on foot, walking a good long league to the
church of Candia, where they placed them. And although this procession was in the month of February, which is the height of winter,
the intemperate weather did not harm anyone. And from the time
the procession started, the saint began to perform miracles, of which
another priest has written very extensively, and for that reason I only
mention it here and shall continue on.

Chapter 4

Sebastián Vizcaíno's Voyage to California in the Year 1596

XII.

During the time the Count of Monterey was Viceroy of this New Spain, His Majesty ordered that the Californias be explored, because His Majesty had been informed that on that coast there were many pearls. This commission was given to Sebastián Vizcaíno, a person worthy of consideration and experience on sea and land; he gathered people for the voyage, and because the religious of my father Saint Francis have been the first in efforts and new explorations, His Majesty ordered them to go on this one, and so Friars Francisco de Balda, as commissary; Diego Perdomo, Bernardino de Zamudio; Nicolás de Sarabia, religious; and Cristóbal López, lay brother, went.

XIII.

Embarking in Acapulco, they began their voyage along the coast of the South Sea, sailing the ship northwest as the coast required. They reached the Puerto de Zalagua,[1] where they stopped and waited for supplies and soldiers. Sailing from here they arrived at the Puerto de San Sebastián and the Islas de Mazatlan where 50 soldiers deserted when they saw the few provisions that they were taking, and suspecting what did happen—that they would have to return for lack of supplies. From here the Friar Commissary, Francisco Balda, returned, and from here the entrance to California[2] begins and is 80 leagues wide. This crossing took them seven days after which they went ashore where there were many naked Indians, pleasant people. From here they went on to another port where they stayed eight days. A religious and 30 soldiers penetrated inland and came to where there were many Indians, but they did not allow the

Spaniards to enter their houses but nearby they brought them a variety of fish, plums, and other fruits to eat, and a few pearls. And then they told the Spaniards to return for they were not to enter their houses, so they did this. The Spaniards affirmed that there was a multitude of people, and that after their fear left them they all came out to see the Spaniards, and the old and young gave them rice. After staying here 15 days, they set sail to look for a more convenient place. The General sent the consort vessel ahead to look for a good harbor and it returned in six days having found a very good one which they named Puerto de La Paz. There are many friendly Indians here who received the Spaniards peacefully, bringing them a few more pearls and different fruits. They entrenched themselves here as well as they could, built a church and some huts for the religious and for themselves. It was the best and most peaceful harbor that they had seen thus far, and so they made it their chief port.

XIV.

The religious asked the Indians to bring their children in order to teach them Christian Doctrine, which they did willingly. They began to teach these children the basic principles but they could not go beyond this since the Spaniards were just there for two months. The Indians had grown to love the priests and they would bring them gifts of fruit; but they fled from the soldiers and disliked them, because they would take away from them whatever they were carrying. They complained to the priests and would point with their finger at the one who had wronged them, and they would tell the priests to remain there alone and the soldiers to go away. This is the incurable illness of soldiers, and woe to the priest who restrains their vices, for then their venomous tongues are against him. *Venenum aspidum sublabiis eorum.*[1] But I take for very blessed those who hear so many infamies because of having reproached vices.

XV.

In this port were found many things of iron, that were left by the vessels of the Marqués del Valle,[1] whom I mentioned before, and they found the military camp set up, and the Indians said that the Spaniards had been there. It is a coast that is most abundant in fish; it rains in October as in Spain, there are many mountains and good timbers to build ships.

XVI.

From here General Sebastián Vizcaíno dispatched Admiral Lope de Argüelles with his consort vessel and a launch, up from the mouth of California to explore the rest of it; they went up as far as a full 30 degrees latitude, and were always well received by the Indians. The coast is very mild, there are many pearl fisheries, and in four fathoms deep, the water is so clear that from above the pearl oysters can be seen on the bottom as clearly as if they were above the water. The Indians gather an infinite number of these oysters to eat what is inside, and they throw them into large bonfires to roast; there they open them and burn the pearls, of which there are some very large ones, and if the pearl is very thick, they pierce it through the middle and hang it around their necks for adornment.

XVII.

Fray Bernadino de Zamudio told me that the Spaniards took out very good pearls, until Sebastian Vizcaino ordered that all of those who took them out should show them to him, in order to set aside the King's portion,[1] and with this they refused to look for any more. I shall not tell here of deaths nor of events for the sake of shortening this account, since I am not writing a history. I only say that the land seemed very good to everyone, and if they had not needed supplies, they would not have returned, and today all that land would be very well settled. God knows what is best.

Chapter 5

Sebastián Vizcaíno's Journey
to Cabo Mendocino

XVIII.

Some vessels coming from China and the Philippines, in north latitude 42 degrees saw the termination of the mainland that was formed there, which they named Cabo Mendocino,[1] in honor of the Viceroy Antonio de Mendoza,[2] who had sent them, and they saw that from there to the Puerto de la Navidad, it was all mainland. When they reached New Spain they told this to the Viceroy, who sent out an expedition to explore all this coast up to it; he sent a few vessels, and they did not go beyond the Puerto de Santiago, which is now called Puerto de Magdalena, in latitude 25 degrees. They turned back because it seemed to them that it was impossible to continue ahead because of the northwest winds, which are continuous on that coast. It is a *viento catanero,* diametrically opposed to navigation, since it blows along the coast from the northwest.

XIX.

King Philip III learned that his father had ordered this exploration to be carried out. His Majesty also found some papers and reports that certain foreigners had given to his father, in which they tell him unusual things that they had seen in that land, carried there by the force of the storm that they experienced while they were fishing for cod in Terranova,[1] and they went from the North Sea to the South Sea by the Strait of Anian,[2] and, at least, if it is not the Strait of Anian, it is the outlet of a strait which came out beyond Cabo Mendocino, in 43 degrees latitude. On this strait they had seen a most highly populated and rich city, well surrounded by walls, and whose people were civil, courteous, and well-mannered. And there were other things worthy to be seen.

XX.

His Majesty ordered this exploration to be carried out, not sparing any expense, since it was his will. The Count of Monterey, wishing to attend as soon as possible to what His Majesty so fervently had ordered, named as General of this expedition, Sebastián Vizcaíno; as Admiral, Toribio Gómez de Corban,[1] and not wanting to give them friars from this province, he took three discalced religious of Our Lady of Carmen,[2] named Fray Andrés de la Asuncion, Fray Antonio de la Ascension, and Fray Tomás de Aquino. Gerónimo Martin [Palacios] went as cosmographer for mapping the land. They left Mexico City on the 7th of March, 1602. On the 5th of May, three vessels and one barge for entering the coves, left Acapulco; and several set sail and headed to the northwest. It has already been said that the winds are contrary to this navigation, and for this reason, from the time that they left the Puerto de Acapulco until they reached the Cabo de San Sebastián,[3] which is beyond Cabo Mendocino, the voyage lasted nine months of continuous navigation. They reached the Puerto de la Navidad, and the Cabo de Corrientes and the Islas de Mazatlán, these are two medium size islands and between them and the mainland there is a good harbor, into which empties a copious river[4] that comes from Nueva Galicia. Here is where the Englishman, D. Tomás Cadi,[5] repaired his ship while our ships from China, for which he was waiting to rob, were arriving. On the mainland by this island is Caponeta[6] and Chametla. From here the entrance to California begins along the coast, and the mainland of this New Spain, and 34 leagues from these islands, toward the region of Sinaloa, the Rio de Toluca flows into the sea, which there they call Río de Narito.[7] They left here crossing an arm of the sea between these islands and the Cabo de San Lucas, which is next to and part of the mainland of California. Here the crossing is 60 leagues. Next to Cabo San Lucas is the Puerto de San Bernabé where there were a great many naked Indians, with bows and arrows. Generally these are the weapons all over the land, and this fact is so for the entire journey. These Indians called the Spaniards to come ashore, they went ashore and when the Indians saw so many Spaniards, they withdrew to a hillock; and as the Spaniards kept on approaching, they kept on withdrawing. Fray Antonio de la Ascension, for whom they waited, went up to them, and embraced them with great love, and then they placed their bows and arrows on the ground. This priest called a Negro to take a basket of hard biscuit to give them, and the Indians were very happy to see the Negro, and they said that nearby there is an island of Negroes and that they are their friends. On this shore there is a great quantity of pearl oysters, here they caught a great quantity of fish such as ruffles, porgy, sea bass, *cornudas,* topes, sharks, devilfish, rays, *chuchos,* river fish, salmon, horse mackerel, little bass, mutton fish, striped tunny, dolphins, flounders, *ciruelos,* small lizards, and other varieties whose names they did not know.[8] On all this coast there is a great quantity of sardines; it is a healthful, good, and fertile land with good climate. There is much game and bird hunting, many groves and fruit-bearing trees, the Indians brought many animal skins to sell, tanned on the flesh side, these were lion, tiger, wolf, and coyote skins. And they brought many neatly made small cotton nets.

XXI.

The consort vessel left this place and came to the Puerto de la Magdalena, and they did not see the other vessels until they reached the Isla de Cedro. They ran into great storms on this voyage; every day they considered themselves lost; I shall only tell here about the things that they saw, for brevity's sake. This harbor of Magdalena is extremely large, and has a most beautiful bay, fine shelters; it has two entrances, and an arm of the sea extends far inland; it was not learned how far inland it reached; it is densely populated by Indians.

XXII.

This is the place where the Englishman, who took the vessel

Santa Ana, threw the people who were on it on land, and, after having sacked her, set fire to her.[1] They left here and sighted a bay, into which a river emptied; the name of it is Ensenada de San Cristóbal; they arrived at the Bahía de Ballenas, named thus because of the great number of whales that are there. There were many Indians who said that farther inland there were greater numbers of them. They reached the Islas de San Roque, then the Islas de la Asuncion, Esterio, and Mala; there was a great number of sea lions as large as calves. There is an abundance of fish. They left in search of the Isla de Cedros, and came upon a high mountain, against which the sea beats, completely bare, without any grass or trees, all of it marbled with bands of various colors, so perfect and striking that it caught the eyes of all, because one could see the rock formations from afar. Some miners who were along said that it was a great wealth of silver and gold, and they tried to get ashore; but the coast was so wild, and the waves were beating with such great force, that they were unable to do so. They reached the Isla de Cedros, entering between the mainland and the Isla de Navidad. The consort vessel and the frigate, before reaching the Isla de Cedros, anchored in the Puerto de San Bartolomé, which is dry and without water; all they found was bitumen that smelled like shell-fish and because it did not have a good odor, they did not load any aboard; some affirmed that it was ambergris and there was so much of this substance that they could have loaded an entire ship with it, for all the shore was filled with this bitumen, and let no one be surprised at this, because there are so many whales there, and the surge of the sea throws this ambergris on the shore; there was also a vast amount of fish ashore, because in fleeing from its adversary, which is the large fish, they come so close to shore, where the other, being large, cannot reach, and the waves of the sea easily cast them ashore. And for this reason, on the coast there are innumerable birds drawn by the odor of the fish. They explored this land and as they did not find water, they left as soon as they could; they reached the Isla de Cedros, next to which is a point called Cabo San Agustín. The frigate went to sail around and measure the Isla de Cedros and found that it was 30 leagues in circumference with great pine forests on the crests of the highest hills; all of these were exceedingly tall cedars. There are many Indians but they refused to make friends with the Spaniards and rather threatened them with their arrows. The frigate went to explore the cove and they saw that an arm of the sea flowed far inland, they did not see the end of it since it flowed very far inland toward the east. They went in search of the Isla de Cenizas[2] steering to the northwest which is toward the mainland; they reached land which was good, beautiful, cheerful, and well wooded. They saw the Bahía de San Hipólito,[3] good, peaceful, and fertile, and found a wide and direct road that led inland, and a large ravine covered with palm leaves. It would hold more than 50 persons. Four leagues to the northwest is the Ensenada de San Cosme, a good harbor, sheltered from the northwest wind. Near the shore, on the mainland, is a large fresh water lagoon. The land is good and fertile, well-wooded, and filled with a multitude of people. They reached the foot of a great, high, black mountain range, cut into the sea, named Sierra de San Cipriano. Next to these mountains, on the leeward side, which is the southeast, are some white barrancas and among them a multitude of people. Next to it is the Isla de San Gerónimo. They reached the Bahía de San Francisco, where there were many friendly and peaceful Indians. Here they found bison and elk horns. The land was extremely good, well-wooded, and gave signs of having an abundance of cattle because of the great amount of dung and tracks that were seen. Beyond this place is a small bay into which the flood tide of the sea enters with great fury, and when the tide ebbs it remains the same. In this port and in that of San Gerónimo, there were great numbers of horse mackerel and many different kinds of fish. The frigate entered this bay and found an excellent harbor. They went ashore and there were many Indians fishing in rush canoes, and as soon as they saw the Spaniards, they came toward them with joy and they gave them some of the fish that they had, with great love and good will, and then they told them where there was good fresh water. These people showed special affection toward the Spaniards and they would not return to their ranchos without bidding them farewell and asking their permission to go and rest; and from farther inland many Indians came to see the Spaniards. The women were modest and dressed in animal skins. The Indians here trade in fish with the Indians of the interior; they take fish and bring back *mescalli,* which is a preserve made from the roots of the maguey. The Indians here said that inland there are many white people, clothed and bearded, and that they had arquebuses and that it was only six days' journey from there. They cannot be the soldiers of New Mexico, for according to the demarcation of the land, by the variations of the meridians and claims on the maps, according to what the cosmographer indicated, it is from there to the Spanish headquarters in New Mexico 200 leagues. Fray Antonio de la Ascensión says they are Russians.[4] Departing from here, they reached the Isla de San Hilario, then there is a large bay that gives shelter from the northwest wind; there were many Indians who were very bald; from here they left, sailing against the wind and the currents; they reached a large bay surrounded by high mountains where through a gorge an arm of the sea entered. Near here are two islands to the west, called Todos Santos. Six leagues beyond are four islands called Los Coronados.[5] North of these islands on the mainland is the Puerto de San Diego; it has woods that ward off the northwest wind, it has many oaks, reeds, broom, rosemary, and many aromatic herbs. The harbor is extremely beautiful and large, and provides shelter from all kinds of weather. On the other side to the northwest there is another port.[6] On this shore they dug some holes in the land, and when the tide was out the wells had fresh water in them, and when the tide was in, salt water. Many Indians covered with blue and silver came to see the Spaniards; being asked by signs what that was, they showed some ores from which they made their paint, and they said that some bearded white men who were living near there, were working that material. Coming up to a Spaniard who was wearing a leather jacket trimmed with beads and braid, they said that those white men also had some of those leather jackets. This port is fertile, with many pastures, good lands, much hunting of birds and beasts, good climate, an open sky and good soil. They reached a cove, a good stretch of land 12 leagues away from the mainland, it is called the Isla de Santa Catarina,[7] and before reaching it, they sighted indistinctly another larger one, to the southwest of this one of Santa Catarina. The inhabitants of the island rejoiced greatly over the arrival of the Spaniards. They are fishermen, using boats made of planks with a high bow and stern and the middle very low, some will hold more than 20 persons.[8] There are many sea lions which the Indians hunt for food and with the tanned skins they cover themselves. The women are handsome and modest, the children are white and blond, and very happy. Among these Indians, many of them wanted to come with the Spaniards, they are that affectionate. From here one follows a straight and orderly chain of islands which are from four to six leagues distant from one to another. All these islands together are 100 leagues long and they all communicate with each other and also with the people on the mainland.

As these islands are so many, so thickly wooded, and so large, those mariners who come from China have always taken them to be the mainland, and so they always steer away from them. Between them and the mainland is a channel 12 leagues wide called the Channel of Santa Bárbara which extends from east to west. When they arrived at the entrance of the channel, which is near the mainland, a canoe with four oars came out from land, and in it came the lord or petty king of that coast. This canoe reached the consort vessel and, as the ship had been sailing with a favorable wind, the canoe circled it three times with the greatest speed. The Indians were all singing in the tone that the Indians sing in their dances. They came on board and, without fear, the petty king went up and walked around the drill deck three times singing. Then, having done this, in the presence of everyone, he gave a long discourse and when he finished, he told by signs that the people of the Isla de Santa Catarina had been telling him for four days in their canoes that those bearded white men, goodhearted and friendly, had arrived. They had also given them many presents, and for that reason he was coming to offer them his land and whatever was in it; and since he did not see any women on the ship, he asked about them, with signs so clear that he made himself understood as well as if he were speaking Spanish. They told him that they did not have any, then he asked them again to go ashore, that he would remedy that need, and he promised to give 10 women to each Spaniard. They laughed over the offer. The petty king, thinking that they were making fun of him and that they believed that he would not keep his word, told some soldiers to go ashore in his boat, and he and his son would remain as hostages, and they would see how he would keep his word. It was already night-time, and so, they put off going ashore until the next day, and they sent him away with many presents that they gave him. Within an hour the southeast wind came up and as it was astern, they did not want to lose the chance. At dawn, they found themselves at the last islands of the channel, which are six and they are two leagues from each other. The channel is 24 leagues long; the coast of the mainland is beautiful, cheerful, wooded, and has a multitude of people. They left these islands and went on to the mainland to examine it closely. It was high and hilly, and in its shelter there are some coves. From one of them there came out four canoes and in each one there were two Indians who came up to the ships and gave them a great quantity of fish, and many salted and preserved sardines. The Spaniards gave them a few trifles, and then they returned. They came near a lofty mountain range that was red on the slopes and very white on its summit; it is called Sierra de Santa Lucía and it is the one where the vessels from China make their landfall; four leagues beyond, the Río del Carmelo empties into the sea among rocks, it flows down from some high white mountains; on its banks are many white poplars and black poplars, willows, *carsas,* and many other trees of Spain. Two leagues beyond is another excellent harbor;[9] between it and the river there is a pine forest which is two leagues across. The land forms a point at the entrance of the bay: it is called Punta de Pinos, the harbor is called Monterey.

XXIII.

The fleet entered this port on December 16, and from here they sent the consort vessel with a message to the Viceroy, giving him an account of everything that had been discovered, with a map of the entire coast, with its ports, and islands, and their locations. The General sent for help in order to finish exploring California, into the gulf, and to put an end to the doubt of whether it is a bay or a strait that has an outlet into the North Sea by the coast of Florida, as the Indians affirm. The General wrote to the Viceroy that by the month of May of the following year he would be expecting reinforcements in California, at the Puerto de la Paz.

XXIV.

This Puerto de Monterey is extremely good, it is protected from all winds, it has deep water, much firewood, and good timbers to build vessels, there are oaks, rockroses, broom, wild roses, black-berry bushes, willows, poplars, springs of fine water, and extremely fertile pastures; good land for farming; there are many good animals and some are very large: there are bears so large that their paws are one third of a *vara* long and a span wide;[1] there are some animals whose feet are round like a mule's and whose horns are like a goat's, these they say are elk; there are other animals as large as young bulls, with the form of a stag, and the cleft foot of an ox, hair like a pelican's down, about a span long, with a long thick neck and nape, and on their heads long antlers like a deer, with a tail about one *vara* long and half a *vara* wide.[2] There are deer, rabbits, stags, hares, wild cats, turtledoves, thrushes, sparrows, linnets, cardinals, quail, partridges, robins, wagtails, cranes, vultures, and pelicans. There are birds with the form of turkeys and they are so large that their wings [when spread out] are 17 *palmos*³ long from the tip of one wing to the other. The coast has all kinds of fish and shellfish that are found on the coast of Spain, there are many seals and many whales, this harbor and its environs are heavily settled by very friendly and generous Indians, who like to give what they have; they were very sorry that the Spaniards should depart from their lands, because they had grown very fond of them. They are Indians who have a government. The consort vessel and the frigate were here until the third day of the month of January of the following year of 1603.

XXV.

They left in search of Cabo Mendocino; the consort vessel entered the Puerto de San Francisco,¹ to see if it could find any trace there of a ship named *San Agustín*,² which was driven to shore in that bay, the year 1595, and which by order of His Majesty and the Viceroy D. Luis de Velasco, Governor Gómez Mariñas had dispatched from the Philippines to carry out this exploration of which we are giving an account, and which was driven to shore in a storm. The consort vessel anchored behind Punta de los Reyes, which is a point that forms the harbor; no one disembarked, because a great storm had caused the frigate to drift, and they knew nothing of where she was. The consort vessel came within sight of some high red mountains, and 14 leagues beyond to the northwest they saw a cape cut into the sea and near it some mountains covered with snow, by the landmarks and latitude they said it was Cabo Mendocino, which is in 42 degrees.

XXVI.

When the frigate had weathered the storm, the pilot checked the latitude and found that they were in 43 degrees; the land forms a point that was called Cabo Blanco, from which the coast continues to the northeast; at this point was found a very abundant and deep river,[1] along whose banks there were large ash trees, willows, rock-roses, and many trees of Spain; they tried to enter, but the strong currents did not permit it, and seeing that they were in a higher latitude than their instructions ordered, I should say destructions under such circumstances, they turned back toward the Puerto de Acapulco. But let them do whatever the occasion and weather permit, and whatever might be fitting, holding a council among themselves of what is important.

XXVII.

They say that this river continues on to the great city of Quivira,[1] which is the city about which the foreigners told His Majesty, when, because of the weather, they went through the Strait of Anian, and from which account His Majesty ordered this exploration to be made.

XXVIII.

General Sebastián Vizcaíno returned to California. He did not wait there for the help as he had planned, because he barely had any sailors to man the sails, for, besides the many who had died, all the rest of them were sick, and so he came to the coast of this New Spain, to see if perhaps its climate would bring health to the sick men, as did happen, for as soon as they arrived at the Puerto de Mazatlán, they all recovered their health; and since at that time the government of Peru was given to the Conde de Monterey,[1] he neither sent the help, nor has anything more been done about this voyage, and thus everything has remained in silence.

XXIX.

In confirmation of the existence of this great city of Quivira, is an account which was given by Pilot Morera to Rodrigo del Río,[1] a former governor of Nueva Galicia, which account says: "While two Spanish ships in Terranova[2] were fishing for cod, such a great storm came upon them that it carried them through the Strait of Anian,[3] and one of them, being carried along in the current in spite of itself, entered the mouth of a copious river which is in the same strait toward the southern part; this vessel came to a densely populated city surrounded by gates and walls; eight sailors disembarked with their arquebuses and when they came near the city, the Indians did not allow them to enter inside, although they received them peacefully; nearer to the city, a little more than the range of an arquebus shot, was a spring of lovely water, and there close by, a small house, they told the Spaniards to go in and rest, and so they did this for three days, and were generously feasted with chickens, corn, tortillas, different fruits, and chestnuts and many other things. At the end of this time the king wanted to see those foreigners as something that had never been seen; such a crowd of people came out that they filled those fields, and finally they brought the king, carrying him on a litter made of a yellow metal, and the king wearing his crown and dressed in animal skins; and when the king came to a place where he could see and judge the features and figures of the Spaniards, they stopped the litter, though they did not place it on the ground, but carried it the way they had been, and they told the Spaniards to come out of their lodgings so that the king could see them. The Spaniards wanted to go up to the litter where the king was in order to greet him. The natives made signs to them not to approach, but for them to remain standing; they did this and the king kept looking at them most attentively, and after a while the Indians made signs to them to go into their lodging again and then the king returned to the city. The Indians kept on regaling the Spaniards as they had been doing. The Spaniards lost their fear, and as the women went to this spring for water, one of the Spaniards tried to force a woman inside the house. She went away to complain to the city, and then many Indians came to tell the Spaniards to go back on board ship immediately. When those who had gone returned they told the rest of their companions what had happened. Besides having experienced great shipwreck, these ships were burdened with so much ice and cruel cold that most of the men were frozen, others became ill, so that almost all of them perished. Those who escaped, seeing that only a few remained to go to Spain, reached Florida, where the most observant one, in order to give an account of these things, embarked on a frigate that was coming to this New Spain. When he arrived at the Puerto de San Juan de Ulúa,[4] he became deathly ill, and knowing that his days were at an end, he called the head brother of the hospital, and had him write this account, so that a thing like this might be known, as worthy to be seen." The man died, and they sent this account to Rodrigo del Río.[5]

XXX.

According to the indication I am sure that this is the same city that had been seen by the one who discovered Anian and notified His Majesty, and that it is the same that was seen by land by the 30 men whom Francisco Vázquez de Coronado sent from the plains of Cibola.

XXXI.

And although some conscientious ones have notified His Majesty of these things, they have not noted how and by what route this exploration is easy, because experience always teaches us new things and one goes on forever learning more about this land; and so I say that this exploration from the Puerto de Acapulco is to labor in vain, because of the causes that have already been mentioned of contrary winds, and in order to explore the rest of California, one ought not to enter it with a vessel of great burden, because it has many shoals and reefs in the middle of the gulf and because there is great danger of being lost; the important thing is that in Sinaloa they should construct four long vessels with their decks, which is easy to do, since they can use oars and sails, and they are easier to handle and can enter all the coves to see what is there, without running into a storm and in any entry they can be sheltered and protected.

XXXII.

Concerning the exploration of the great city of Quivira, it should be explored from one of two places, either by way of the mainland of New Mexico, or by two vessels leaving Florida, and entering the Strait of Anian. I am not saying that soldiers should leave Florida by land, although it is mainland joined to this one, as I shall explain finally as opposed to unbelievers who affirm to the contrary, because it is swampy and is far from this city, by all calculation. So if one is to enter by land it must be by way of New Mexico, and if by sea, it must be by the coast of Labrador, which is in 50 degrees latitude, and not by way of Acapulco, for it is impossible to explore it from there; and if this city is explored, two things will result; one, the welfare of souls; the other, the profit to the royal crown, and that His Majesty may enjoy as many riches as they say are there; for since he is such a good Christian, he will use them so well, in sustaining these beliefs.

Chapter 6

D. Juan de Oñate's Entrance
into New Mexico

XXXIII.

D. Juan de Oñate[1] left this city of Mexico the year 1596, taking in his company 10 friars of my father St. Francis, men of great spirit and letters; their names were Alonso Martínez, commissary of this expedition; Francisco de San Miguel, Francisco de Zamora, Juan de Rosas, Alonso de Lugo, Andrés Corchado, Juan Claros, Cristóbal Salazar, (priests); and Juan de San Buenaventura and Pedro de Vergara, lay brothers.

XXXIV.

D. Juan de Oñate took more than 700 men from here in New Spain, for this expedition, the flower of the Chichimeca military, and other important persons; moreover, as on such occasions, there are never lacking those who are envious or those with evil intent; these men succeeded in upsetting this expedition, which caused great trouble and detriment to this gentleman's estate and great loss to that land on account of the delay of the *Visita,*[1] that caused him to be delayed there three months while fully ready. More than 200 men turned back and many of them married men and, because of such a great delay, their estates were destroyed and consumed and so they remained behind. Leaving long accounts aside, which is not my intention, I say that D. Juan Oñate entered that land with more than 400 men; the 130 married ones with their families. When they had traveled 400 leagues, straight north, toward the North Pole, in 37 and one-half degrees latitude, they reached the valley of the Teguas Indians, who are settled on the banks of the river which the Spaniards call Río del Norte[2] because it flows from that direction. He established his camp between this river and the Zama,[3] partly because he wanted it there, and because some men with bad intentions have lied about it and defiled it, just for the sake of speaking evily of the pueblo that D. Juan de Oñate founded,[4] saying that it is bad and poor land. These are men who escaping have left fleeing, and when they are asked the cause of their departure, so as not to confess their crimes, tell these stories, defaming the land; and contradicting them, I say that this pueblo is very important and of very great moment and usefulness to the entire land, when and if the rest is settled. Since the plan of D. Juan de Oñate was to form expeditions and to explore the land, he could not find a more convenient situation than this place, because of its being in the center of the realm, and because to the west of it California is 200 leagues away, as has already been seen, and to the east, Florida is about 300 leagues air distance, since we ought not to measure it by the distance that Orantes,[5] Cabeza de Vaca, nor Hernando de Soto traveled, since they all wandered around lost, walking back and forth, and I am only calculating diametrically to the north. The arm of the sea named Río San Lorenzo,[6] an easy embarcation point for Spain, is about 100 leagues away, for as I shall mention further on, this river empties out at Labrador, on the boundary of Terranova, where every year they come to catch codfish, and thus, for this reason, it is the best port that could have been chosen, and the Indians here were peaceful. In all the provinces the people are pleasant, settled, and they helped the Spaniards with their supplies and appeased their hunger, and they helped them to build their houses, and everything else, and of course they gave their allegiance to His Majesty. Concerning the quality of the land, it is cold and healthful, with the climate of Spain. Its healthfulness is attested by the fact that the Indians reach the age of more than 100 years, for I have seen them. It is a fertile land with fine crystalline waters and much major and minor livestock is raised, and if it were not for the greediness of the governors who have taken them all out to sell, the fields would now be covered with them. A great supply of wheat and corn and all kinds of vegetables is gathered. As far as saying that it is poor, I answer that there never has been discovered in the world a land with more mines[7] of every quality, good and bad, than in New Mexico; there are mines in the mountains of Socorro, in the salt beds, in the mountains of Puaray,[8] in Tunque, at the entrance, in the *siénega;*[9] in San Marcos, in Galisteo, in Los Pozos, in the Picuries; in this pueblo there are garnet mines, in Zama, and in all the mountains of the Hemex,[10] there is nothing but mines. Here I discovered many and inspected them for His Majesty, from which I took out 18 *arrobas*[11] of metals. When I returned I divided them among all the camps through which I passed, in order for everyone to see the metals of New Mexico. More than anything else, there are mines, and there is no place that does not have them; the Spaniards who are there are the poor ones who have no means to work them and they have less enthusiasm, and are enemies of all kinds of work, and in the land we have seen silver, copper, lead, magnet stone, copperas, alum, sulphur, and turquoise mines that the Indians work with their talent, since for them, they are diamonds and precious stones. The Spaniards who are there laugh at all this; as long as they have a good supply of tobacco to smoke, they are very contented, and they do not want any more riches, for it seems as if they had made the vow of poverty, which is a great deal for being Spaniards, who because of greediness for silver and gold will enter Hell itself to obtain them.

XXXV.

I will prove this truth, so that no one will doubt if his enthusiasm is that weak, and I say; it was about nine years ago that three Flemings, residents of this city of Mexico, named Juan Fresco, Juan Descalso, and Rodrigo Lorenzo, very honest men, straightforward, and exemplary, went into that land to look for mines. They found many mines and made many tests; they took out silver for we all saw them, and they returned to this New Spain to buy implements and equipment; they took a miner and a refiner and returned the second time. The day the news arrived at the town of the Spaniards that these Flemings were returning to work the mines, that same night they set fire to the workshops in which the ores were to be worked which had been built since the time that D. Pedro de Peralta was governor,[1] because he was interested in this, and with his litigations all of this ceased. With this, one sees their depraved intention and that it still troubles them. They are enemies of silver and do not want anyone else to mine it.

XXXVI.

The Indians of those provinces are settled, their houses are large, I mean to say, they have many rooms and many stories; they dress in blankets of cotton, which is abundant in the land. They paint these blankets; they also use buffalo hides and wolves skins, and feather blankets, for which they raise many turkeys. There is no difference in the men's clothing and the women's; they all wear shoes because of the cold; their food is corn, beans, squash, plants, which all of them store up for the winter ahead, before the colds begin; venison, hares, rabbits, wild chickens, quail, partridges; they also kill bears to eat, for there are many, and much fish. *Bagres*,[1] pike, trout, and *matalote*[2] are the most common throughout the Río del Norte, so that they do not die of hunger. One thing is to be praised about these nations, and it is that they are not drunkards, nor do they have any beverage except river water; they observe well the things of the church and they obey the religious who teaches them the doctrine. With this, all has been told concerning everything that is in New Mexico. After the Adelantado[3] D. Juan de Oñate had put things in order and had inspected what there was in all the settled and surrounding nations, he endeavored to make explorations inland; I will give an account of those that produced some result.

Chapter 7

D. Juan de Oñate's Journey
to the Great City of Quivira

XXXVII.

The Adelantado D. Juan de Oñate left the town of New Mexico to explore the great city of Quivira, the year 1599; he took on this journey Father Francisco de Velasco, who at that time was commissary of the province, a very learned and apostolic man, and for his companion, a lay brother named Fray Pedro de Vergara, and 80 soldiers; he took as his guide, a Mexican Indian named Jusepe, who had gone inland in the company of Humaña,[1] and this Indian with two other Mexicans escaped after Humaña had taken the life of Captain Leiva, a Portuguese national, and a very brave man. The Indians of the interior had already killed Jusepe's two companions; he escaped as best he could. Later D. Juan de Oñate found this Indian in New Mexico in the pueblo of the Picuries, and he guided this D. Juan de Oñate in the direction and route that he had entered, which was across the buffalo plains, where no one can die of hunger because of the innumerable buffalo herds that are there; the plains are so extensive that no one has seen their end and conclusion. They traveled to the eastnortheast, and saw great grazing grounds, beautiful fields, a great deal of water, fertile land for farming, and a good climate. Afterwards they continued going up to the northeast, traveling, by their calculations, 200 leagues, uphill and downhill and not in a straight line. They reached the fertile promised land, where the fields, of themselves, without any cultivation, produce grapes, plums in great abundance and many other fruits. Although there are Indians on these plains they are not settled in any definite place; they have small straw huts. We call these people *vaqueros*[2] because they sustain themselves with this livestock; they neither sow nor harvest food, they tan the hides and take them to sell at the settlements and with them they trade for corn flour, and in this way they sustain themselves.

XXXVIII.

The Spaniards encountered the Encansaques Indians[1] who were going to fight with their enemies, the Quiviras. The hostile Encansaques began to do much damage in the settlements, some of them setting fire, others seizing houses, Fray Francisco de Velasco, being so Christian and pious, was moved by compassion because of the destruction that those Indians were causing, and begged the Adelantado to come to their aid in so much destruction; this stirred up the Indians and they turned against the Spaniards, much to their sorrow, for among them about a thousand died, and of the Spaniards, not one was dangerously hurt, although many were wounded. In this place they say that they killed Humaña and his companions when they were returning loaded with gold;[2] here were found remains of this, for some articles of iron were found, some *botas,* and the bones of the horses; the way they killed them was to set fire to the camp while they were resting. Only one Spanish boy, named Alonso Sanchez and a partly burned mulatto woman escaped. When this expedition was made, they say she was alive and that she was three days' journey from this pueblo. This Alonso, the Indians told me, was alive a few years ago and because of his great courage, was a captain, and very feared by the Indians. They also learned that near there, were seven small hills on a plain, from where the Ahijados[3] take out the gold which they refine. Nothing was done about any of this.

XXXIX.

They also say that the Quiviras had sent an ambassador to welcome the Spaniards, but since they saw them in the company of their enemies the Escansaques, they were afraid. The ambassador did not dare to cross the river that separated them from the Spaniards, but the Adelantado sent some soldiers to try to catch him from behind, as was done and they put him in irons. He was an Indian of importance; moveover, the Indians were more astute mustering out falsely while the Spaniards were getting their arms, they took care to carry off the prisoner still in irons, as he was. Since that land seemed to be densely settled, as the innumerable fires demonstrated, the Adelantado ordered some soldiers to go inland. They traveled one full day and returned to say that they had not come to the end of the settlement, and the Indians had said that it was very large and that farther to the north there were other larger ones; they say also that if when the Indians hung their clothes on the trees to fight, they had looked at their clothes, they would have found two gold goads of the lances with which they fight, and the large golden cups from which they drink. Nothing of this was seen.

XL.

These Ahijados have a great amount of gold which they work and which they call *tejas*. Besides as a proof that there is much gold, and that they esteem it and work it, I do not need any other witness than what everyone saw in this city of Mexico and in the court, and the fact is that in the aforementioned fight with the Escansaques, the Adelantado captured two Indians of the Ahijado nation. One was a little boy, and the other was a lad; when they baptized these two, they gave them the name of Michael, because the battle had been on Saint Michael's Day. Well, this Indian Michael built the furnace in which the gold is smelted with such excellence that those who understood this process were amazed, and he did not know any metal but gold, because he said: "In my land there is nothing else but this and so, I do not know the others." The silversmiths in Mexico could not deceive him with gold-plated things nor alloys nor other metals.

XLI.

They took this Indian to Spain so that His Catholic Majesty,

King Philip III, could see him; the silversmiths of the court tried to deceive him with a mixture of all kinds of chopped up metals, and they could not, because he would recognize at once what was pure gold. In the house of the Duke of the Infantado there is a map that this Michael drew, of all those kingdoms and provinces of his nation, and the surrounding ones with as great skill as a cosmographer could. It is sufficient to say that Fray Francisco de Velasco saw it as a witness. This Michael made known in the court so much concerning the majesty and power of his kingdom and of the great riches of gold that exist there, that His Majesty, knowing that the Indian was not lying, ordered a thousand men to make ready for this exploration. The gentleman who had taken the Indian to Spain for the sake of performing a greater service to His Majesty, said that he wished to furnish half of them at his expense, which would be 500 soldiers. The offer seemed very good to the king and he wrote to the Viceroy, that when this gentleman had given and fulfilled what he had promised, that another 500 men should be gathered together at his expense [the king's]. Since he did not fulfill his promise because he was unable to do so, neither did the king, and so this is the way this expedition has remained, until God moves the heart of some rich man who may want to spend money in order to leave a memorial.

XLII.

And coming back to continue with my account, I say: that the Spaniards went back towards New Mexico along the same route on which the Quiviras had fled from that settlement and who from fear had absented themselves and deserted their houses. They also returned to them, and seeing the great killing among their enemies, they realized two things; one, that the great destruction of their settlement had not been done by the Spaniards, but by their enemies; the other, that the Spaniards were very courageous and good to have for friends, and so the news of their great courage was spread throughout all the interior, and desiring their friendship and contact with them, they sent from Quivira an Indian ambassador of high standing and seriousness. He had with him 600 servants with bow and arrow, who served him; the neighboring Indians, hearing the troop that was coming, announced that it was coming to do away with all the Spaniards, and they even said the number of people was great, later the contrary was seen; but in the meantime, God knows how the Spaniards' hearts were. At last the ambassador arrived and gave his message, inviting the Spaniards with his friendship and lands so that they would help them fight against their enemies, the Ayjaos, who are the ones that possess the gold. The Adelantado did not have the forces to go there, because while he was away on this journey many of the soldiers that he had left in the town to protect that haven, had escaped from him. The conversations, questions and answers were all in the Apache languages for they (the Spaniards) understood it very well. He told many things about his land, about the lord of his kingdom and about the great abundance of gold that there is there. D. Juan de Oñate, in order to assure himself concerning what the ambasador said and in order to know if it was true that they knew what gold was, melted a gold chain and a bar of lead, another of copper, another of silver, brass, metal, iron, all these metals together; he called the ambassador and the rest of the Indians, although not all of them together, but in troops at different times, and asking them which of those materials there was in their land, they all indicated the gold, and said that was what there was and that the rest they did not know. Those who did not recognize it at once, took the gold in their hands and smelled it and by the smell they knew it immediately; and so, there was not an Indian who failed to know it, and they said that their king had a great amount of it. The Adelantado asked them that if there was as much gold as they said, how was it that not one of them was carrying even a grain of it. The ambassador answered that his king has placed great punishments on the one who takes it out of his kingdom, and the person who breaks this law is immediately impaled; but if they had known that the Spaniards prized it, they would have brought some.

XLIII.

This ambassador said that the Spaniards had traveled a great deal out of their way on the route that they took, that if they had gone directly north, they would have arrived quickly; and so, according to what they said, one should go by way of Taos and through the lands of the great Captain Quima, across those plains. Proceeding with his mission and seeing that the Adelantado was not disposed to go there with him he told him to give him 12 soldiers and he would go very contented. The Adelantado said that he could not. Then the ambassador said how was he to go before his king with such a poor answer, and for him to give him at least six soldiers, that with those he would go very contented. The Adelantado promised them to him and he named them, and he ordered them to make ready with provisions, and to prepare arms and horses. With this, the ambassador left very happy to tell the news, leaving two guides to lead him [Oñate] by the direct route, but after the ambassador had left, they changed their minds and these soldiers did not go, for if they had gone they would have obtained clarification and this doubt would have been solved, whether it exists or does not; here a very great opportunity was lost, and we can say that it will be long before the lost opportunity will be recovered.

Chapter 8

*D. Juan de Oñate's Journey
to California by Land*

XLIV.

In the year 1604, on the seventh day of the month of October, D. Juan de Oñate left the town of San Gabriel to explore the South Sea; he took in his company, Fray Francisco de Escobar, who was the commissary at that time of those provinces, and a lay brother named Fray Juan de San Buenaventura, apostolic men. The friar commissary was a very learned man who had the gift of languages, for he learned all of them with great facility. On this expedition Oñate took 30 soldiers, most of them being raw recruits; and they took only 14 pairs of horse armor. Having traveled over that western region 60 leagues, they reached the province of Cuñi which is on some plains that are more inhabited by hares and rabbits than by Indians. There are six pueblos, and in all of them there are no more than 300 terraced houses with many stories, like the ones in New Mexico. The largest pueblo and the head of them all is the pueblo of Cibola, which in their language is called Havico; it has 110 houses. Their food, as is common all over the land, is maize, beans, squash, and game. They dress in blankets made of *iztli,*[1] woven of twisted cord; these Indians have no cotton. They left this pueblo, and after having traveled 20 leagues between northwest and west, they reached the Moqui[2] Province. Here there are five villages and in all 450 houses; the same number of houses and of cotton blankets.

XLV.

In the Zuñi province[1] there are silver mines of such a blue color that they use it for paint and take it to the settlements of New Mexico to sell. I brought some stones to show and the painters told me that it was the best blue in the world, and that in this city of

Mexico each pound of it was worth 12 pesos and not a pound was to be found. Likewise in the green (paint) of New Mexico, especially that of the Hemex,[2] the gold leaf is extremely fine, and of those two materials, one can bring abundant loads here.

XLVI.

They left Mooqui, and after 10 leagues to the west they reached the Río Colorado;[1] they named it thus because the water is almost red; this river flows from southeast to northwest, then it turns to the west, and they say it flows into California. From here to where it empties into the sea there are more than 100 leagues of pine forests. From this river they traveled to the west crossing a mountain ridge of pine forests which was 8 leagues across, and along whose southern side the Río San Antonio flows. It is 17 leagues from San José, which is the Colorado, and it flows from north to south through rough mountains and extremely high rocky cliffs. This river has very little water and a great quantity of very good fish; from this river on, the climate is moderate. Five leagues ahead to the west is the Rio del Sacramento which has as much water as the San Antonio and it has as much fish and as good. It has its source 11 leagues to the west; and flows from northwest to southeast, along the slopes of some very high mountains where the Spaniards took out some very good ores, and where there are many mineral deposits. The Spaniards had not found anything that pleased them until they reached this place. It is a very fit place for the Spaniards' dwelling; and is a place where many skills can be carried out, there are good lands for farming, beautiful fields and pastures for livestock, and an abundance of water. In these mountains the Cruzados Indians[2] have their dwellings; they are rancheros and their houses are made of straw. They do not plant their food, they sustain themselves with game that they kill, deer, and mountain sheep of which there are many. With these animal skins, both men and women cover their bodies; they are all shod, both children and adults. For food, they also have mescali, which is a preserve made from the maguey root.

XLVII.

They call these Indians the Cruzados, because of some crosses that all of them, children and adults, have falling down over their foreheads and are tied to a tuft of their hair and they do this when they see the Spaniards. The origin of this ceremony was not learned then; since then it has become known that many years ago, a religious of my father Saint Francis was traveling through that land, and he told them that if at some time they should see bearded white men, in order that they might not offend or harm them, they should place on themselves those crosses, which are something that they esteem. They remembered it so well that they have not forgotten it. The men are well featured and noble, and the women are handsome and affectionate with pretty eyes. These Indians said that the sea was 20 days' journey from there, calculating that they travel about five leagues a day. It must be noted that not one of these nations has been caught telling a lie. They also said that two days' travel from there, there was a river with a little water, along which they would go to another very large one that flows into the sea, on whose shores there was a nation whose name is Amacava,[1] and then farther on were many other nations that plant and harvest maize, frijol, and squash. They left the Río del Sacramento traveling 15 leagues between the west and the southwest finding good streams all along the way. They reached the river of little water which is called San Andrés; from here on it is *tierra caliente;* there was an abundance of pitaya,[2] and different trees. They traveled along it for 24 leagues and reached the large river that they were looking for, by the description the Indians had given; it is called the Río de Buena Esperanza[3] and when it reaches the sea it is called Río del Tizón. This river has as much water as the Duero[4] and is as gentle as the Guadalquivir.[5] It flows from northwest to southeast, then narrows through some high mountains that cross it, and past these narrows, it flows from northwest to southwest, having along both sides extremely high mountains which run parallel with it, and all along the banks there are wide lowlands.

XLVIII.

Another day after having arrived, the Adelantado sent Captain Gerónimo Márquez[1] with four soldiers up the river to explore this nation of Amacava Indians. In a short time he brought two Indians whom the Adelantado regaled and he sent them to call the rest of them. They said that they would do it and that they would bring something to eat. The following day, the Adelantado seeing that the Indians were preparing loads, ordered that 12 soldiers prepare themselves to go for food to the settlement; but before the soldiers had gone, more than 40 Indians had arrived bearing maize, frijoles, and squash; and then an Indian named Curraca, which means Lord in their language, stood up and gave a long speech, making it understood what everyone presumed, that he was pleased to have seen the Spaniards, and that he wanted their friendship.

XLIX.

Here was where they had the first news of the Laguna de Copalla,[1] from where, it is presumed, the first Mexicans who settled this New Spain left. In glowing words, they described this lagoon and its lands and all its shores as very settled. And one Indian said "Copalla" very clearly. Captain Gerónimo Márquez told me that those Indians, on hearing a Mexican Indian, the servant of a soldier, speak, one of them asked, "Where is this man from? Is he perhaps from Copalla?"[2] Because that is the way those from there speak; and besides, these Indians said that those of that language wore gold bracelets on their wrists, on their upper arms and on their ears, and that they lived 14 days journey, of those they traveled, from there. They indicated that these people were between the west and the northwest. The Indians also told the Spaniards

that they could travel along this lowland as far as the sea, and that it
was a ten day journey of those they traveled and that it was all settled.
This river is navigable. They left this place and traveled five leagues
without seeing any Indians, because the mountains were very rough
and the road very close and narrow; but past this narrow place the
lowland becomes wide and highly settled. Here an equal number of
Indians as in the previous rancheria came out to receive the Spaniards with food. They all belong to the same nation. Asking them
where the sea was, they said that it was nine days' journey down the
river, but that if they would cross the river, it was only four. This
river they were following on the north bank, and they were traveling
to the northwest. The Adelantado did not think it a wise thing to
stop following the river downstream, and so he continued traveling
along its lowlands, always seeing many Indians, and asking them
all about the sea, that they now knew was named *Acilla,* and they
would all answer motioning from west to northwest, north, northeast, east, and they said that the sea turned around that way, and
was quite near. They said that from the other side of the river, it
was only four days' journey away, and that the Gulf of California
is not closed but is an arm of the sea which is a part of the North
Sea and the coast of Florida. All the Indians along this river are
comely and well featured. The women are handsome, and whiter
than those of New Spain, being people among whom the men go
naked and the women cover only their private parts. Whenever
these Indians travel they carry a lighted firebrand in their hand,
which is why I believe that it must be called Río del Tizón; thus
a soldier on this expedition who had gone with Sebastián Vizcaíno
to California affirmed, and he said that Vizcaíno had gone in search
of the Río del Tizón, and I believe that if he had reached it, he
would not have turned back as he did for lack of food, since here
there is a great deal.

L.

Having left this nation of Amacabos,[1] of which as well as of the others, they saw only what was on their route, they reached the nation of the Bahacechas. Their language is almost the same, they are friends and they communicate with each other; the houses of all these people of this river are low, made of wood, and covered with earth. The head of this nation is named Cohota. This man came out with a great retinue to the road to receive the Spaniards and to beg them not to go ahead that day, but to spend the night in their pueblo, and so it was done, to please him. This Indian and his people told of many things and secrets of the land. They asked them about the Laguna de Copalla and he said the same thing that was said before, and showing them a gold toothpick, he kept putting it near his wrist as if encircling it, indicating that the Indians of the lagoon wore bracelets of that material. The Adelantado showed them a coral and asking them where there was any of that, they motioned toward the south, and said that the Indians of the coast took them out of the sea, and that the sea, when it is rough, casts many on shore, and that the Indians dig in the sand and take it out to sell. All the Indians said this about the coral wherever they went, and it seemed to be true, finding much of it in possession of the Indian women.

LI.

Having passed this place, while resting in the pueblo of Captain Otata of the same nation, they asked him and his pueblo some questions and showing them some silver buttons, they affirmed before many soldiers that near there, motioning to the west, there was much of that material and that it is called *ñañe querro*. They showed them a silver spoon, and as soon as they saw it, they said that the bowls and vessels out of which they eat are made of that material, and they indicated that they were quite large and deep. They rolled a silver plate, so that it would make noise, implying that the others sound that way when they fall on the ground, and that it does not break,

and placing a silver plate with water in it on the fire, they said that
in them they cooked meat, where they were motioning, but that the
others, although they were of that (material), were large, and this
information was of their own accord, without anyone's persuading
them. And striking many times as if striking a knife on the plate,
and letting it fall together with force so that it would make more
noise, they said that that was the way the others sounded and that
they were only five days' journey away from there, indicating the
sea on the ground, in the middle of it an island, which they called
Ziñogaba, which is the name of the nation that inhabits it. One goes
by sea to this island in some canoes or boats, and from the coast to
it was only one day of sailing; they leave in the morning, and before
the sun sets, they are already there. They drew on the ground the
size of the boat, marking a line on the earth, and he began to measure
and the boat was 70 feet long and 20 feet wide. And asking them if
that boat had a sail-cloth in the middle of it, the Indian took a stick
and put it in the middle of the boat that he had drawn, and an Indian
at the stern, pretending that he was steering the rudder, then took a
cloth and extending his arms on the stick that he had erected left
running as fast as he could indicating that the others sailed through
the water that way, and even faster. The truth is, that if the Indian
had not seen it, they would not know how to describe it so perfectly.
They also said that all the people of that island wear on their necks
and on their ears, pearl shells which they call *xicullo*. They also told
about an instrument on which they play music when they dance,
which instrument is a long stick which has hanging from it many
pieces of that metal of which they make dishes that they eat from,
and making a great deal of noise at the same time, they dance to the
music.

LII.

With all this information, the Adelantado did not want to fail
to go and look for a port, since the instructions were so easy to under-

stand and with the good convenience of guides who offered themselves for this purpose. After they left this nation of Bahacecha, they reached the nation of the Ozaras Indians, who had quite a difficult language; the Indians here were ill-featured, and less friendly, and from them one can have little satisfaction and less security. These Indians are settled along a large river, although it does not have as much water as the Río de Buena Esperanza, it is named Río del Nombre de Jesús[1] and it flows between barren mountains, flowing from southeast to northwest into the Río de Buena Esperanza, 20 leagues before it reaches the sea. It was learned that all the river is settled by this nation and that multitude is very great. They drew signs on the ground of 20 rancherias or pueblos of this nation. They make cotton blankets, their dress and hair is different from the rest. Their hair is long and they wear it braided and then covered with a cloth or with chamois. On this lowland the river forms many basins. Here they saw some fine sweet acorns, which the Indians said were from the other side of the river, and that there were many. Asking about the source of the Río de Buena Esperanza, the Indians said that it is near the sea toward the northwest, and that from its source to where it empties into the sea, it is 160 leagues long and is all settled, and that at its source, bison and deer as large as horses range, with which fact one can see that it is good level land and has an abundance of water. From this Río del Nombre de Jesús to the sea, it is densely settled, with greater population than had been seen thus far; moreover, the language is like that of Bahacecha, and if it is not the same, they differ very little. Their dress, their way of living, their houses like the others, are well organized and arranged. They all came out to receive the Spaniards, and invited them and offered them their food. Among these Indians were found many white pearl shells, and other very large luminous shells, and they make vises and drills which are very interesting to see. These Indians said that along the coast there were many of those shells to the west, and they motioned to show that behind a very high mountain range, the sea was there.

Along the slopes of this mountain range the Río de Buena Esperanza flows into the sea. From these Indians, they informed themselves again of all the things that Captain Otata had done, and they did not differ in anything, and showing them a pearl, they gave it a name and said that there were many very large ones. And an Indian came up to the Father Commissary and, taking a rosary of very large beads that he was wearing around his neck, he said that there were pearls as large and round as the beads of that rosary. And in regard to the Isla de Ziñogaba, these people said that the ruler or leader of it was a giantess, and that her name was Ziñacacohola,² which means Woman Captain, or Mistress; they described her as being half again as tall as the men on the coast, being as they are, very fleshy and very broad and having large feet. They said that she was old and that she had another sister who also was a giantess, and that there was no man of her kind, and that she did not mix with anyone on the island. The mystery of her dominion on that island could not be learned, whether it was inheritance or tyranny by force of arms. Everyone on the island was bald, since they had no hair on their heads.

LIII.

The first nation after leaving the Río del Nombre de Jesús, is Halchedoma.¹ There are eight pueblos, the first one has 160 houses; it was judged to have about 2,000 souls. I have already said that they saw only what was on their route. Next is the Cohuana Nation, which has nine pueblos, of these a great number, probably more than 600 men and women, accompanied the Spaniards, and spent the night with them. Next is the Haglli Nation. There are 100 [sic] pueblos. Then the Tlalliquamallas, six pueblos. Here more than 2,000 souls gathered when they brought the corn. Then came the Cocapas,² which are nine pueblos, this one was the last that was seen, and it extended to the last place where one can drink fresh water, since it is five leagues from the sea, because at that many leagues the salty sea flows upstream into the river. In the stretch that there is from the

Río del Nombre de Jesús until it reaches the sea, more than 20,000 souls were seen on this side of the river only, for on the other one, they said, they were innumerable and only the fires were seen. The Indians said that they did not cross over the other side, because those were their enemies, although they were the same nation, and that the others came and killed them and did these people great harm. With this, one sees that the others are many. They arrived on San Ildefonso Day at the last place, and the nearest to the sea and the last place where one can drink water. Then the Day of Saint Paul's Conversion, Mass having been sung, the Adelantado and the religious with nine soldiers left and reached a most excellent harbor, which harbor and bay the Río de Buena Esperanza forms when it flows into the sea; we called it Puerto de la Conversión de San Pablo. This harbor is so large that more than a thousand vessels can anchor in it, without disturbing each other; the river is four leagues wide at the mouth where it flows into the sea. In the middle of the mouth is formed a low small island, not of sand, as all the coast is, but the entire little island is made of mud, which is probably about two leagues long from northwest to southeast.

From what could be seen, it forms a great protection to the bay and divides the mouth of the river into two, one to the east, and the other to the southeast, each mouth being more than one and one-half leagues wide. This island guards and protects the harbor from the south, and from the west the harbor is protected by a ridge of mountains along whose slopes the river flows, from almost north to south or from northwest to southeast, and empties into the sea, and a promontory of the ridge extends more than six leagues into the sea. On the east shore this port, or bay, has another range of mountains that extends toward the sea from northeast to southwest. It is seen that seven leagues distant from the bay it ends and terminates in the sea, with seven or eight small hills or hillocks with low promontories; after these on the land side it forms a round promontory that is higher than the others and in which the sierra ends. On the west shore, which is the one next to the bay, it ends with three little hills, or round promontories somewhat higher than the ones of the other range, and the last one of these is higher than the other two. After these toward the mainland there is another elevated promontory, from where the sierra forms a ridge which extends more than 20 leagues from southsoutheast to northnorthwest toward land. The gulf extends along this coast where they were, from east to west, and the promontories of this sierra rounding the capes from the west shore, that, as I have already said, enter into the sea more than six leagues and the gulf extends behind this sierra toward the north, according to what all the Indians said, those of the coast as well as those of the river, for they affirmed that it turns around toward the north, northeast, and the east.

LIV.

The Adelantado, D. Juan de Oñate, took possession of this port in the name of His Majesty, and he gave it to the Father Commissary, Fray Francisco de Escobar, in the name of His Majesty, in order that our sacred religion may settle and so that it does settle that land and the others next to it and near it, and so that we may turn our attention to the conversion of the natives, in the place and places that are most fitting to our way of living.

LV.

We took possession[1] of this place on the 25th day of the month of January, day of the Conversion of the Apostle Saint Paul, patron of those provinces, and guardian of New Mexico, the year of Our Lord 1605, for the honor and glory of God Our Lord.

LVI.

When this was done, the Adelantado and those who had gone with him, returned to the camp so that the rest of the soldiers could go and testify that they had seen the sea and thus it was done, taking four days to do this. Some soldiers affirmed that they had seen tuna and that they were acquainted with them because they [the soldiers] were men from Spain. Having seen this, they returned over the same route on which they had gone, being as well received by the Indians and with the same friendly treatment as when they had first arrived. Having reached the Ozaros Indians, as they had already informed themselves of the rest of the nations, they all said that this nation extended very far along the coast, and that these are the ones who gather the coral from the sea, which they call *quacame*. Endeavoring to gather some, he found a few pieces and they said that because they were far from the coast, they did not have many. Farther along on the Río de Buena Esperanza, among the Indians of this nation, a few others were found; but in the Zuni Province more were found and they bartered, and they said that the Indians of the valleys of Señora[1] brought them there to sell, and that they are only seven days' journey from there, and that these people gather them from the sea and that they were not far from the sea, and that this nation extends that far, which sea they indicated was to the south and southwest. From the province of New Mexico as far as the sea, Fray Francisco de Escobar found that just along the road there were 10 different languages; this religious was so skillful and he had such a memory, that wherever he arrived, he learned the language immediately, and so on this return journey he spoke with all the nations, and they all understood him. They reached the Bahacecha Nation, where on their first arrival there, Captain Otata and the rest had given so much information about the land, about the Copalla Lagoon, and about the gold, and the Isla de Oro y Plata; questioning them again they said the same thing as when we first arrived there, without changing it in any way. They performed the same activities that they had done when we were there before, with the silver plate, as has already been told; they added only that this silver they took out of the high part of a hill that was on the other shore of the island, behind which the sun disappears when it sets, and they said that they cut it with a hard instrument. When asked if it was made of the same material, they said no, and they made it understood that it was a dark yellow material, and showing them a small plate of brass, they said that it was not made of that; and when they saw that they were not understood, one of them got up and went to the Adelantado's kitchen, and picked up a copper ladle and said, that like that was the instrument with which the metal was cut and of which they make the bowls and cooking utensils. They left here and Captain Otata went out to the road to receive the Spaniards with a great retinue and tumultous ceremonies as is their custom, throwing their bows and arrows on the ground. He gave the governor a string of white beads that he was wearing around his neck, and another one to the Father Commissary (for among them it is a great gift) which he had sent to barter for with some cotton blankets to the Isla de Ziñogova, which on their former journey there, the governor had given him for himself. It is very apparent that the island is nearby, since he had gone and returned in such a short time. They examined them again about everything, and they did not contradict themselves in anything.

LVII.

These people told about many marvels of nature that God had created between the Río de Buena Esperanza and the sea, which has caused disbelief in those who heard them, and so when we see them, we shall swear that they are true; that is the way it is, and in the meantime, I shall not say anything about them and I shall go on in silence. And in order to finish this account, let me say: That after having endured many hardships and great hunger even to the point of eating up the horses, concerning which so as not to lengthen this account I shall not tell everything; they reached the town of San Gabriel on returning, the 25th of April of the year 1605, and everyone was well and healthy with none missing. There they rested, and were as well received as they were wanted.

Chapter 9

Florida, Terra Firma with New Mexico

LVIII.

Contrary to unbelievers who do not want to believe that Florida is terra firma with this one (Mexico) and with New Mexico, knowing as it is known, that men have come overland from there, and so I shall give an account of everything that has been seen along the coast and terra firma, although the people of Florida are not the ones who have seen the most; for the English have seen more than we have. Since Juan David,[1] Englishman, in the year 1586, reached as far as 72 degrees where he found the sea frozen, because of the great cold, and he hurried away for if he had not found this impediment he would have reached a higher latitude.

LIX.

Another Englishman, named Hudson,[1] in the year 1612, reached 65 degrees latitude by the same route. He entered through a bay that the coast forms in 60 degrees. It flows to the west more than 300 leagues farther, and then to the south for more than as many more.

LX.

At the entrance to this bay, Henrico Hudson, Englishman, arrived the same year of 1612, from which it is seen that they have more curiosity than we (have).

LXI.

On this basis I say: that the most northerly part of the Indies is from Totila, as far as the border of Guadlancha and from Guadlancha this coast extends 200 leagues to the Río Nevado which is in latitude 60 degrees.

LXII.

From the Río Blanco to the Bahía de Maluos it is 200 leagues, this is named the Costa de Cabo Labrador, it has to the south the

island that they call Los Demonios in 60 degrees. On this coast of
Labrador, the natives are comely, great workers, they are dark, and
great hunters. They dress in tanned white animal skins; there are
large and very dense forests, and in them many wild animals, grif-
fins,[1] bears, lions, and one must consider something, and it is, that
all the terrestrial animals, and all the birds are white. All the men
and women wear silver and copper pendant earrings. They all paint
their faces for ornament, a common custom of all Indians. They are
idolators and fierce. Many Bretons and some from Norway have
gone over to settle this land, many went in company of Sebastián
Gavoto,[2] pilot and great cosmographer, and many Englishmen have
gone over also, who have remained there and settled.

LXIII.
From Maluos to the mouth of Marco it is 60 leagues. It is in
latitude 56 degrees. From Marco to Cabo Delgado is 65 leagues, it is
in latitude 54 degrees.

LXIV.
From Cabo Delgado the coast extends more than 200 leagues
toward the west, as far as the Río San Lorenzo, which is the river
that I mentioned before to the north of New Mexico a little more
than 100 leagues; this they call by another name, the Strait of the
Tres Hermanos. In this place a square gulf is formed, and it extends
down from the San Lorenzo as far as the Cabo de Bacallaos,[1] more
than 200 leagues according to the information of the Río de Buena
Esperanza Indians as was reported in the journal of D. Juan de
Oñate. This strait is the one that they say comes out of the North
Sea and flows into the South Sea.[2] Between this cape and Cabo Delgado are many well settled islands, they are called Cortes Reales;[3]
these islands are owned by the French. The Islas de Corte Real,
Valle, Duxchastous, Cabo Despoix, Cabo Breton, where there are
many Frenchmen from Brittany, with these islands the gulf of San
Lorenzo is hidden.

LXV.

The Cabo de Bacallaos is in 48½ degrees; it is as cold as Flanders because of being in the same clime, which is 48½ degrees. Here the French abandoned a fort because they were unable to stand the cold which was unbearable. From here it is 70 leagues to the Bahía del Río, which is in 45 degrees. From Terranova to Florida it is 900 leagues.

LXVI.

From the Bahía del Río to the Bahía de los Isleos it is 70 leagues. It is in latitude 44 degrees.

LXVII.

From Los Isleos to the Río Fondo, situated in latitude 43 degrees, it is 70 leagues.

LXVIII.

From the Río Fondo to the Río de las Damas which is in the same latitude, it is 70 leagues.

LXIX.

From the Río de Gamas [sic][1] to the Cabo de Santa María, it is 50 leagues.

LXX.

From this cape to Cabo Bajo it is 50 leagues.

LXXI.

From Cabo Bajo to the Río de Santa Ana it is 100 leagues.

LXXII.

From the Río de Santa Ana to the Cabo de Arenas, which is in latitude 39 degrees, there is a bay 80 leagues long.

LXXIII.

From Cabo de Arenas to the Puerto del Príncipe it is 100 leagues. This place is named Chicoria.[1] The inhabitants of this Chicoria resemble giants, and the king was marvelously large. They are swarthy and mulatto-like; they are idolators, although they believe that the soul is immortal and that there is a Hell or place of suffering in very cold lands, where the gods permit them to purge their sins in order that their souls may later rise to Heaven, which is in a temperate climate. They also believe that many people live in Heaven and below the earth, and that under the sea there are gods. In this province there are misshapen pearls, precious stones, and silver. Herds of deer graze in the fields as rams and ewes do here. They make cheese from does' milk.

LXXIV.

Adjoining this province, in the same latitude, is the province of Guadalupe. It has the same things and advantages as Chicoria.

LXXV.

From the Puerto del Príncipe to the Río Jordan, it is 70 leagues; in this center of the realm the Río Negro is situated. Eighty leagues to the mountains is the Diamond Mountain, near which Ensign Moyano[1] arrived and took some Indian women to Florida. They were so beautiful that all of them married the Spaniards of Florida.

LXXVI.

From the Río Jordan to Punto de Santa Helena it is 40 leagues. It is latitude 32 degrees.

LXXVII.

From Punto de Santa Helena to the Río Seco, which is in 31 degrees, it is 40 leagues.

LXXVIII.

From Río Seco to La Cruz it is 20 leagues.

LXXIX.

From the mouth of La Cruz to Cabo Cañaveral,[1] it is about 80 leagues, and in between are situated the Bahía de Bajos, the Bahía de Ballenas, the Bahía de Osos, the Bahía de Santa Catarina de Quale [Guale],[2] the Bahía de Epoquache, [Espoguache], the Bahía de Pala, where today one sees the site of a fort that belonged to the English.

The Bahía de Reynoso,[3] by another name Guadalquivi(r), for any galleon, however large it may be, can enter it. The shoals of this bay extend 2 leagues into the sea, the Bahía de San Pedro, the Bahía de Santa María de Sena, and the Bahía de San Mateo, where Pedro Melendez [Menéndez] Márquez[4] killed the Frenchmen.[5] Twelve leagues from this one is the Bahía de Matanzas, where he killed Juan de Ribao,[6] uncle of the Queen, Doña Isabel de la Paz, who was the wife of his Majesty, Philip II. Our presidio is here in 28½ degrees, today the Presidio de San Agustin on Cabo Cañaveral, where they usually inspect the fleets that sail out of La Habana, 38 leagues, in latitude of 28 degrees.

LXXX.

From the Puerto de Espíritu Santo to as far as Moscoso,[1] it is 9 leagues. Here the Adelantado, Hernando de Soto, made port, and from here he went inland in the year 1539, with 900 soldiers that he had with him, and he saw the following, until he died in the endeavor, as will be seen further on. From Moscoso to Iribaracusi it is 17 leagues, and 26 in total. Three leagues from this village there is a bad swamp, with a lagoon one league wide and very deep. On its shores it has a great deal of mire, and is 12 leagues long. Six leagues distant from them there are many valleys of very fine cornfields which the Indians plant. This fertile land is called the province of Aquera.[2]

LXXXI.

From Aybibaracusi[1] to Aquera, that is now called Santa Lucía, it is 20 leagues, extending north and south; the people are already Christians. From Vitachucu to Ozachile, it is 10 leagues, and it is level land, and one crosses a large river. There are 12 leagues of wilderness.

LXXXII.

From Ozachile to the Cabo de Elas there is a very large lagoon, although it can be forded.

LXXXIII.

From the Puerto de Espíritu Santo to Apalache it is 150 leagues, a shorter route has already been discovered.

LXXXIV.

From the Bahía de Aute to the Bahía de Acuse it is 60 leagues, it is a fine port with good depth as far as the shore.

LXXXV.

From this Puerto de Aute the Adelantado Hernando de Soto sent Diego Maldonado in some brigantines to inform La Habana of what had happened to him in the exploration of the inland. But since on this journey they did not have a pilot for surveying, his account does not tell in which direction he was traveling, and so I do it thus.

LXXXVI.

From Apalache to Apacha it is 20 leagues. The people are peaceful, and up to here they are all Christians.

LXXXVII.

From Apacha one follows a river upstream for 40 leagues, it is good fertile land like the land in Apalache. These people are also peaceful. The Spaniards traveled north-south.

LXXXVIII.

From here which is the Presidio de San Agustín, the route goes directly ahead to Amachava, where there are six villages of Christians. To the left lies Taxichica, which consists of more than 10 villages, and those of the Ocomi league who are all Christians; and to both sides are many villages of infidels, in which villages there is a multitude of people.

LXXXIX.

From Amachava, which is called Santa Helena, to Avacara, it is 12 leagues.

XC.

From San Juan de Avacara to San Martin, where one of the principal Indian chiefs is, it is eight leagues.

XCI.

From here to Santa Fé, it is 4 leagues.

XCII.

From Santa Fé to Claca, it is 16 leagues, and four to the Presidio de Mal Camino. They reached another province that is called Chalaqui, which is very poor in supplies. Most of the people were old and blind, and few in number, it is 20 leagues from Abapache, and they reached the province of Cofaquin. At the narrowest crossing, it is eight leagues, and there is a great wilderness and many arroyos of water and two large rivers. At 24 leagues the wilderness begins and traveling upstream for 12 leagues one reaches the first village, Cofachique. From the end of the desert to Cofachique, it is two leagues and it is on the opposite side of Ayoque, one follows the coast; here there is brass that is more brilliant than gold. Those who understand anything about this science say that it has an admixture of gold. They say that this river comes out from Santa Helena in Florida. Here there are temples where the principal Indian chiefs are buried, an endless number of pearls in a wooden box, and a great deal of misshapen pearls. One league from this town is the head village which is a great town, and the temple where the Indian chiefs are buried has large groves for one league surrounding it. The village is called Tolomeco; the temple is 100 paces long and 40 wide and it has 12 armed giants at the entrance. At each side are six wooden boxes of pearls and misshapen pearls, wooden figures of the dead Indian chiefs and their relatives. There are 88 rooms of arms, with weapons of brass studded with pearls and misshapen pearls. Leaving Cofachique one travels 32 leagues. They reached the province of Chalaqui. From Chalaqui to Xuala it is 50 leagues and from Apalache to here, it is 270 leagues. Through this Xuala, the Rio de Cofachique flows and from the bay of this port, where they disembarked, it is probably 250 leagues to Apalache, which altogether is 400 leagues. From Xuala to the province of Guajule there are 200 leagues of wilderness. From Guaxule to Ichiaha there are 30 leagues, where there is a river like the Guadalquivir when it flows through the city of Sevilla. There are very good pearls here. A soldier opening an oyster took out a pearl as large as a hazelnut that they evaluated at 400 ducats in Spain. This Isla de Ichiaha is five leagues long. They went on from this island, crossed the river, and slept in a village of Acoste[1] where there were more than 1,000 warrior Indians, who are very good people. Coca [Coosa] is a province of more than 100 leagues, all well settled and fertile. This village of Coca is at the extreme end of the province; it has more than 500 houses; here the Indian chief lives, and the Spaniards left them a statue of Christ. An escaped soldier who deserted, whose name was Falco Herrado, remained, along with a sick Negro. The last village is Talici, and then, 8 leagues farther on, one enters Tascaluca after crossing the Talesfe, a large river. They entered Tascaluca where the Indian Chief was a giant and so was his son. There was not a horse that could support him; only a very heavy horse could support his weight. Here the Indians killed two soldiers. From here it was a league and a half to Mauvila.[2] At this place more than 10,000 Indians suddenly attacked the Spaniards who arrived first, and they killed some of their horses and robbed everything that was in their camp. This village was enclosed by extremely thick timbers that were about three *estados*[3] high; they were tied and plastered with mud, they had their embrasures, and there were only two gates. They fought inside with such fury, that they made those on horseback retreat more than 200 paces, since from the fence they would throw a great deal of stone at them and they did them much harm. So they retreated in order to attack better, and fought for nine hours; they came out of it with 1,600 serious wounds, without counting the ones of little importance which were an equal number. Eighty-two soldiers and 45 horses died; more than 10,000 Indian men and women died, for the women also fought with great spirit. Here the flour, the wine, the altars, the chalices, and the sacred vestments were burned. Mass was no longer said, not a thing was left, except what they were wearing; everything was burned in the houses. They made a vestment of chamois and celebrated dry Mass, saying the prayers, they adored the cross which the priest raised in place of the Host. This lasted for three years, until they left for Christian land.

XCIII.

From this land of Mauvila to the Puerto de Acusi, which is to the east north-northeast, it is 30 leagues, where the vessels from La Habana that were coming to look for them, had arrived. In this province they punish adultresses severely. They left this province of Tascaluca where this Mauvila was situated and where the bloody battle took place, and they left Azunde. Having traveled 12 leagues they entered Chicaza,[1] and saw a company of more than 1,500 Indian warriors, who crossed in canoes to block the way, and on the other side there were also more than 8,000 Indians, and two leagues distant there were many of them scattered around, everything to block the way of the Spaniards; however they crossed after traveling 16 leagues. They reached the main village, Chicaza, where there are many walnut trees and many fruit trees; the village has 200 houses. In these very secure quarters, the Indians fell upon the Spaniards; some came to fight, others were burning the houses. They fought for two hours; 40 soldiers and 50 horses died; 500 Indians died. They left Chicaza and fought the Fort of Alibamo,[2] which had four walls, each one 200 feet long. More than 2,000 Indian men and women died. From Alibamo to Chisa there is a wilderness 16 leagues long. Chisa is on the banks of the largest river that was seen. From Chisa they left for Casquin which is upstream and where they found a crossing, in which there were many canoes. On the opposite bank there were more than 6,000 Indians to block their way. When they had traveled 16 leagues they reached Casquin; these Indians asked them to perform a ceremony because it had not rained, they did this and set up a cross, and immediately it rained and abundantly. The clergy and the friars went on singing the litanies, and placed the cross on a high hill that was next to the river. They left Casquin for Capaja, it is 12 leagues away. This place is divided under two Indian chiefs, and is situated in a large swamp and lagoon, which after crossing there are very fine pastures. Then eight leagues beyond are some hills, from which can be seen Capacha; 40 leagues from Capacha there is crystalline salt, and there is very fine brass; the land, when it is to be found, is sterile and very poor, and so they returned to Casquin. From here they traveled 36 leagues over fertile land that was thickly settled; they reached Quiguate, from which the province takes its name. They traveled 24 leagues downstream from Casquin, reaching Colima, where they were received peacefully. The principal village is half a league away; here they found a great deal of resistance, even the women fought, and they would let themselves be killed before surrendering. Four women attacked a Spaniard, and with blows and bites they had him almost dead, until a soldier arrived, and with dagger he killed them because they refused to let go of him, and an Indian split the round shields of two soldiers and wounded them very severely. Another Indian attacked a Spaniard on horseback, and with a blow, opened his horse from the top of his head to his chest with a hachet that he took away from a soldier, and another one (an Indian), with one blow of a stick, knocked all the teeth out of a soldier. They all paint themselves in order to appear more ferocious. They flatten their heads with boards from the time they are babies, and some of them are more than half a *vara* long, pointed toward the top. Here they stayed 20 days curing the wounds from three cruel battles that they had with them. They traveled two days and left this province, they reached Utiange and traveled four days through good fertile land, but sparsely settled; they arrived at this village, which is the head village, the Indians absented themselves and refused to appear, or to make friends with the Spaniards. They have good features. There were many raisins and dried plums, many walnuts and many other fruits. The village was fenced with wood and had rivers on either side, many rabbits, hares, and deer. Here they wintered, and it snowed so much that for more than a month and a half they could not go out to the country. They had enough maize for the entire winter and much firewood. They were here for five months; here Diego de Guzman remained living in concubinage with an Indian girl, the daughter of a chief. They traveled through the province of Naguatex and reached the province of Guacane. They crossed through it in eight days and no more in order not to fight with the Indians: there were crosses on the houses, for the news had spread of the good that they had received from the cross when Alvaro Núñez Cabeza de Vaca and Andrés de Orantes[3] and their companions had gone through. They went through curing the sick with the sign of the cross, for good example produces this much good fruit. These men had gone through here 20 years before the Adelantado Hernando de Soto had, which is the journey of which I am telling.

XCIV.

We left here crossing seven small provinces toward the west, and reaching the provinces of Amilco, they traveled 30 leagues and reached the nation that is on the banks of a river which is larger than the Guadalquivir. The Indian chief was waiting for the Spaniards with 500 warriors but they did not fight. After traveling four days they reached the province of Guachoya, traveling through wilderness.

XCV.

Here they bury with the Indian chief who dies all those who were most dear to him and whom he loved in this life; children, wife, relatives, friends, and servants, are all buried alive with him.

XCVI.

From Guachoya, by long days' marches, they traveled to the west more than 100 leagues after the Adelantado Hernando de Soto had died; here they wandered around lost because their guide was already dead. On the third day they reached the plains of Cibola, where they satisfied their hunger with the abundance of buffalo meat. The Indians of these plains do not have houses but huts; they do not plant grains; they sustain themselves with what they kill with their arrows, and with plants, roots from trees and other things.

XCVII.

These and the Apaches are one tribe, as has been said above, and this proves that Florida and New Mexico are all terra firma with this country where we now are, since the plains of Cibola begin to extend toward Florida at 20 leagues from the settled part of New Mexico, and many times it happens that in dry years these cows go as far as Las Salinas, which is the settled part of New Mexico, belonging to the Tompiro Indian nation. And it is evident to us by what has been seen from New Mexico, that these plains of Cibola are inhabited by Apaches, whom we call *vaqueros* because they subsist on these cows. Therefore these soldiers were not far from New Mexico.

XCVIII.

From here these soldiers turned back with very great difficulties and assaults by the Indians, who killed many of their soldiers. Of more than 60 Indian servants in their service not one was left, and 100 Spaniards and 80 horses reached the Rio Grande[1] and they lodged themselves in Amnoya, from where they set out with the intention of going to Mexico, and they had to return. Here, Juan Ortiz, their interpreter, and 150 persons died. Here they found 20,000 bushels of maize and many dried fruits. This river overflows its banks every 14 years because of the heavy snows that melt in the mountains. It is more than 500 leagues long from its source to where it empties into the sea, which is, according to calculations, where the

English are now, and which is called Bahía de Santa María, el Jacal, otherwise New Virginia, New France. They call it Virginia because in their language it means Paradise.[2]

XCIX.

Here there are more than 25,000 English and French; along three rivers they have three forces; 12 leagues inland they have a very great city in latitude 43 and a half degrees, they extract very rich ores and they take them to England to be worked.

C.

These soldiers embarked on Saint Peter's Day, on rafts, to go downstream; they left Amnoya. On the second day, more than 1,000 canoes attacked them, and killed 48 of their soldiers. These canoes carried 25 oars on each side and in each canoe 30 archers; 350 horses were embarked and in the last village they were all killed with arrows; they kept following them downstream for 15 days, the river was more than 15 leagues wide at this place. After 20 days they sighted the sea, and followed the coast as far as Panuco.[1] Here I shall bring this account to an end because they had already gotten out of so many dangers and afflictions. And if at some time someone should enter this land, with this account he will know the names of the nations, and the order in which they are found, and which land is settled country and which is uninhabited and desert.

CI.

To others, a book of this expedition and conquest of Florida will probably seem an old affair, because it is so long and takes one away so far from here. I confess it, and anyone else will admit it to me, that there is a great difference in having seen it in a history book which is more than 400 pages long, than to have summed it all up in no more than four pages, and which at least has been difficult to sum it up merely to please the reader.

Chapter 10

An Account of the Mexican Nation that Settled This Land of New Spain

CII.

What has been traced and is known to be true is that the Mexican Indians who settled here in New Spain left the Laguna de Copalla, which is 14 days' journey from the other side of the Río de Buena Esperanza;[1] it is more than 400 leagues distant from this City of Mexico straight ahead, for if one goes by way of New Mexico it is more than 540. The straight route is to go in by the valleys of Señora[2] without reaching the Río del Norte,[3] cutting directly to the province of Mooqui [Moqui], and from there to Los Cruzados [the Crossed Indians], and then to continue up to the head of the Río de Buena Esperanza. If one goes from New Mexico on this exploration, one ought to go by way of the Río de Zama[4] traveling to the northwest. That is what the Indians of New Mexico told me when I questioned them.

CIII.

In the journey of D. Juan de Oñate to the Californias, I noted that an Indian was found who on hearing another Indian speak in the Mexican language [Nahuatl],[1] said that was the way the Indians of the Laguna de Copalla spoke. I also said that I would later write the information that they learned on this journey and I would tell it briefly. I touched upon it and continued on with what I had begun, and now I say that the following facts were learned.

CIV.

On that journey were found many ancient buildings and ruins, irrigating ditches resembling those of ancient times in Mexico at Azcapuzalco,[1] and the residue of the metals that they worked. This was seen beyond the province of Mooqui, and asking the Indians what those ruins were, they answered that it was a tradition of the old people, whom they heard tell that many centuries ago a great number of people had passed through there, who had come out of the Laguna de Copalla, although they called it by a different name since they speak another language, to settle in new worlds, traveling to the south. And that they went so far away that nothing was ever known about them, whether they were alive or dead. All these signs and remains of ruins, which are ditches, and residue, are found in the valleys of Señora, Sinaloa, Culiacán, and as they indicate, it is the direct road that they followed when they came to settle this land.[2]

CV.

It is also an ancient tradition among the Indians, that a piece of virgin iron which is three leagues from Santa Barbola, half a league away from the road over which the carts that go to New Mexico pass, is a memorial of the coming of the Mexicans [Aztecs] to settle this land, and that they stopped there, and the idol that spoke to them told them that that iron should remain there as a memorial.[1]

CVI.

The iron must weigh over 800 quintales,[1] and they say that a demon in the form of an old Indian woman who was very wrinkled brought it on her back.[2] Some feat for an old Indian woman!

CVII.

This is something that all of us who pass by that road go to see out of curiosity.

CVIII.

A blacksmith from Santa Barbola split it a little on one side, and others not believing it to be a movable object and brought from afar, but suspecting it to be a virgin iron mine, dug a tunnel underneath it, and the iron, not having the ground on which it was resting, became tilted, and so it is now, tilted to one side.

CIX.

Fray Francisco de Velasco,[1] the gifted priest of whom everyone knows and who has been mentioned before, told me, when I
talked to him about this journal, that while he was going with the
Maestro de Campo, D. Vicente Saldívar,[2] to explore the South Sea,
when they had returned at the end of four months of searching,
without reaching the sea on this journey, reaching the nation of the
Cruzados Indians, some horses were lost; and two soldiers and a
Mexican Indian, servant of a soldier, went to look for them. Asking
some Indians if they had seen the horses, one of them answered
in the Mexican language that he had not seen them. Asking this
Indian where he was from, since he knew how to speak in the
Mexican tongue, he replied that he came from inland, motioning
toward the north, which is where the Laguna de Copalla is. With the
task of looking for their horses, they overlooked taking this Indian
to the camp for everyone to see and question; and later, endeavoring
to look for him, he did not appear, for he had hidden.

CX.

While I was endeavoring very hard and extraordinarily in New
Mexico to ascertain and to verify this truth of whether there are
Mexican Indians there, Captain Gerónimo Márquez told me that the
first time he was at the Peñol de Acoma, entering an estufa [kiva]
which had some Indians painted on the walls, and recognizing
them to be Mexicans because of their dress, he asked the Indians who
those were who were painted there, and they answered that a few
years ago some Indians with that dress had come through there from
the sea coast, and as something never seen among them, they painted
them, and that from there they [the Indians] had gone toward the
pueblo of Cia [Zia] of the Queres nation. With this information I
tried very hard to find out, and asking the head captain of the
pueblo of Cia [Zia], named D. Andrés Pachete, and other old people,
if they had heard anything about those people who had come from

where the sun sets, he replied that he had, that he remembered very well having seen them, and that some of them had been in his house as guests, and that this happened a few years before the Spaniards settled in New Mexico, and that if I wanted to find out about it, that I should ask the Indians of the Hemex [Jemez] nation, in whose pueblos they stayed resting for a longer time.

CXI.

I endeavored to obtain this information from captains of the Hemex [Jemez] nation, and calling the head captain of the pueblo of Amoxunqua, named D. Francisco Guaxiunzi, and the head captain of the pueblo of Quiumziqua, named D. Alonso Piztazondi and D. Gabriel Zandú, his brother, and other people, they all said that it is true that those strangers had been there a few days resting, and that whenever they heard me speaking with an Indian in the Mexican language they would remember the strangers, since they spoke in that manner, and that they still remembered some of the words that they heard them speaking in the Mexican language, and they repeated them to me.

CXII.

The Hemex Indians in their language call these Mexicans Guaguatu, Gauputu, and when I asked the Indians why they give them this name, they answered it was because of their way of living, since they do not have terraced houses like those of New Mexico, but shelters covered with straw, and they do not have *estufas* for their winters, so they had told them, and that over there where they were living it is not as cold as it is in New Mexico, and that afterwards they returned to their land, not by the road over which they had come but by way of the Río de Zama upstream; traveling to the northwest according to the straight route that they indicated to me.

CXIII.

I told these Hemex Indians that if I should find guides I would willingly go to explore this nation since I love them so much, and

because I know their language so well, and that in this way it would
be easy to convert them to the true knowledge and to the body of
the church. They replied that to go directly to the Laguna de
Copalla, a guide was not necessary. One only had to leave by way
of the Río de Zama, and that after having passed the nation of the
Apache Indians of Nabaju [Navajos][1] there is a very large river[2]
that flows into this lagoon. The river is all that is needed for a guide,
and that all the land was level with good pastures and fields, between the north and the northwest. They said that it was good, level,
and fertile land and that there are many nations. The province of
Quazuala, the Qusutas,[3] and farther inland another settled nation
who have stone steps to go up into the houses, of which they learned
all these things from the Apache Indians and others who had seen
all that world.

CXIV.
This is what I have succeeded in finding out about the Mexican
nation. May God permit the door to be opened to such a great harvest for the good of those souls and for the glory and honor of God
our Lord.

CXV.
Eighty leagues before reaching New Mexico on the western
side, two days' journey from the Río del Norte[1] and the *camino real*,
one hears about many pueblos of advanced people who plant cotton,
maize, and other vegetables; who weave blankets, the finest and
thinnest of that kind that have been seen and of which I attest since
I happened to get a few. I obtained them solely to bring and show
them in this country. They say that the land is level, fertile, and has
an abundance of water; this nation is called Los Cojoyas.[2] Up until
now it was suspected that they were the same as the Gorretas[3] Indians, since for a few years some of them have been leaving the area
in company of the Gorretas Indians, who enter and leave New
Mexico, and come to see the Spaniards. On this last expedition when

I left that land, I endeavored to find out what nation it was, and thus it was learned now that they are Cojoyas, their neighbors to the east are the Gorretas, to the south, the Conchos, who are their enemies, since the Indians of El Ojo Caliente,[4] whom they thought until now were Tepeguanes,[5] are Conchos; and the Conchos extend still beyond, for they go as far as the boundaries of these Cojoyas.

CXVI.

In the valley of San Martin, 50 leagues beyond Santa Barbola, while I was showing these blankets to some Concho Indians from Encinillas who came out to the road to see us, and who, since they were Christians baptized by the hand of the holy Fray Alonso de la Oliva, as soon as they saw the blankets, they knew about them and said that it was not far from there where they wove those blankets. They motioned toward the straight and open road which was the *cañada* of this valley of San Martin straight ahead to the north, leaving the *camino real* of New Mexico to the right. We learned this from a Concho interpreter who was very skilled in the Mexican language.

CXVII.

This place is very easy to see with two dozen men, and if they are real men twelve are enough. Perhaps that land is important, and all that has to be done is to go on preparing the ground; and the result will be for the good of souls that must be many, since the Indians say that there are more than 40 pueblos.

Chapter 11

*Narrative of the Pilot Morera who crossed the
North Sea to the South Sea through the Strait*

CXVIII.

Fray Antonio de la Ascension, discalced Carmelite religious, one
of the three who went with Sebastián Vizcaíno on the exploration
of Cabo Mendocino, gave me this account as a true fact, and that is
why I write his name here. This is what he tells me:

CXIX.

A foreign pilot, named N. de Morera,[1] who steered the Englishman from the North Sea to the South Sea by the Strait of Anian,
gave this account to Captain Rodrigo del Río, who was then Governor of Nueva Galicia. When Captain Francisco Draque[2] was returning to his country, leaving through the Strait, this pilot who was
accompanying him was very ill and was more dead than alive. And
thinking that perhaps the climate on land would bring back his
health, and like something dead, they cast him ashore. In a few
days he recovered his health and traveled through that land over a
period of four years; he came out at New Mexico and from there to
Santa Bárbara, and then he went on to the mines of Sombrerete,
searching for Rodrigo del Río, and this pilot told him the following:

CXX.

After telling him at length of his many wanderings, he told
him that the aforementioned Englishman, Francisco Draque, in a
stop at the Strait of Anian, had put him on land, because of what
has been told, and that after he had recovered his health he traveled
through different countries and provinces for more than 500 leagues
on mainland, until he reached a place where he caught sight of an
arm of the sea that divides the lands of New Mexico[1] from another
very large land which is to the west, and on the shores of that sea,

there were many large settlements, among which there is a nation of white people who are accoustomed to travel on horseback and who fight with lances and oval leather shields. It is not known what nation this is. The aforesaid Fray Antonio says he thinks they are Muscovites, but I assert that when we see them, we shall know who they are. This pilot said that this arm of the sea flowed from north to south and that it seemed to him that it went on to the north to join the port where the Englishman had put him ashore. He said that on that sea coast he had seen many good harbors and large bays, and that from the place where they had thrown him ashore, he would attempt to get to Spain in 40 days in a good *patache*,[2] and that he ought to go and visit the Court of England.

CXXI.

He offered to take this Rodrigo del Río to the place on the arm of the sea that he had explored, and he said that he would cross it easily to the other side.

CXXII.

This arm of the sea is known to be a fact, it is the one from California called Mar Rojo[1] and the land which is on the other side is the land of the Californias; as it was told to me, I am telling this, without changing or adding a word of my own.

CXXIII.

All these things about the great riches of New Mexico and the interior land, the Spaniards of New Mexico have known, but they do not deserve to enjoy them, because of God's secret wisdom, which we cannot understand. In this, we see fulfilled the prophecy of the saintly Fray Diego de Mercado, religious of this seraphic religion, son of the province of the Holy Gospel, who, when he saw the troop of people going through the pueblo of Tula, at the time D. Juan de Oñate entered to settle New Mexico, said: upon the soul of Fray Diego, (for this was his vow), God certainly does have great riches in these remote parts of New Mexico, but, upon the soul of Fray

Diego, the present settlers are not to enjoy them, for God is not keeping these for them; and so it has been, for all the first people have
died without enjoying them, and amidst great suffering, because
they have always come with these desires and greediness for riches,
which is the reason that they went there to settle, and they spent
their fortunes. God Our Lord, who knows everything, knows when
and how those riches are to be manifested to men in order that they
may enjoy them, for He alone can know this, since this is what He
teaches us: *non est vestrum, non est tempora del momento.*[1]

CXXIV.

And not only have the settlers of New Mexico not enjoyed
riches, but the scourge of God has been on them always, and they are
the most oppressed and enslaved people in the world, for they are
not masters of their wills nor estates, since with ease, and without
their being able to put up any resistence, the riches are taken away
from them by a strong hand, and they are left stark naked and people
elsewhere are prosperous. These are secret judgments of God.

CXXV.

And if all that has been said were not enough for men to be
encouraged to travel far inland in order to see and enjoy as many
riches as God our Lord has in his keeping there, for all the unbelievers who are late in believing, the following case would be
enough for them to realize the truth and come out of their disbelief.

CXXVI.

While he was Superior of the Convento de Quauhquecholan,[1]
the holy man, Fray Juan de Escalona, religious of this province of
the Holy Gospel, one afternoon at sunset and the hour when the
Ave Maria is rung, was with his companions walking through the
patio of the church because of the heat they felt. They rang the Ave
Maria, and everyone knelt down to pray it. When the prayer was
finished, all the religious stood up except for the holy man, Fray Juan
de Escalona, who remained in prayer, for while the others were pray-

ing the Ave Maria, he was carried off in spirit. The other religious, as they knew him and respected him for his holiness, left him and continued walking around the patio again. After a while, the holy man began to cry out saying: *Beati primi, Beati primi.*[2] The religious who heard him were very attentive and careful to see if they could hear some other thing; but they did not hear any more; they were left desiring to know what he meant to say with those words, *Beati primi, Beati primi,* repeated twice. When the ecstasy was over and he recovered himself, the religious asked him what those voices had been. But he refused to say anything, and the religious, after all, since they were curious, were left desiring to know about that mystery. On another day, when the holy man was going to make a short additional confession (in order to celebrate Mass), with one of the aforementioned religious, his confessor begged him earnestly, under protection of the confessional, to tell him what those voices of the night before had been; and the religious replied: "Under the condition, my dear Father, that as long as I live, no one will know about this, I will tell you." The confessor gave him his word that he would not tell it to anyone as long as he [Fray Juan de Escalona] lived, and when this word was given, he said:

CXXVII.

I will tell you, my dear Father, that yesterday afternoon, when we were praying the Ave Maria, God our Lord revealed to me all the riches and worldly possessions that he is keeping in the interior land of New Mexico to the north. It was also revealed to me that some religious of my father, Saint Francis, are to explore it. And as the first ones who will enter there, they are to be martyred. These religious appeared before me and I saw them being martyred in spirit, and because I was joyful to see them suffer martyrdom with so much spirit and courage, I said: *Beati primi, Beati primi.*

CXXVIII.

It was also revealed to me that when this happens and after that land is sprinkled with the blood of these martyrs, the Spaniards will go in there to enjoy the many riches that are there.

CXXIX.

And this holy man, with this good desire, entered New Mexico with the second expedition of religious who entered during the time of D. Juan de Oñate, and he began baptism in the pueblo of Santo Domingo on the banks of the Río del Norte;[1] among Indians of the Queres nation, and in which pueblo he ended the days of his life as a saint. The prodigious things that happened to this holy man with those Indians are many, and as it has already been mentioned, since this is an account and not a history, for the sake of brevity, I shall not write everything that happened.

CXXX.

I do not know, Most Reverend Father, what heart there is so hard, that with these things, does not soften, and become softer than wax and wish to be the first to enjoy such an emblem of martyrdom and glory. For our seraphic religion honors God our Lord so much, and we receive each day so many mercies, from his generous and open hands, that for our sacred religion, and not for another, he is reserving this enterprise to further honor and give divine light to this poor flock.

CXXXI.

I have informed your Most Reverend Father of all these things, with the brevity and best style that the dullness of my understanding and my unpolished language is capable of attaining, in order that you, as a pious father, and on whom rests the welfare of those souls, may open the door and give permission to all the religious who might have the spirit to go apostolically inland to New Mexico and the new world, without receiving pay from His Majesty, but as I say apostolically. For this blessed province of the Holy Gospel has, as it has always had, religious of very great spirit who desire to go among those infidel and barbarous nations, to lay down their lives among them, in imitation of the One who for our love gave up his life on the tree of the cross.

CXXXII.

After I had finished writing this account, the report that follows came to me, with which is confirmed all these truths of this great world of New Mexico, named Greater Spain, which is so large on terra firma, that no other like it has been discovered. Because . . .

CXXXIII.

To the south one can go on land as far as 52½ degrees south latitude, which is the Strait of Magellan, and to the north it has no determined boundary, and it is as though it were unending.

CXXXIV.

This land from north to south is 2,178 leagues long.

CXXXV.

From the east to the west it is 1,277 leagues long, since it is that far from Terranova[1] to Cabo Mendocino. Thanks be given to the Most High who created it. Amen.

Chapter 12

*Account of the Saintly Mother María de Jesús
Abbess of the Convent of Santa Clara of Agreda*

CXXXVI.

It is very probable that in the pursuit of the exploration of New Mexico and conversion of those souls, they will soon come upon a kingdom that is called Tidam, which is 400 leagues from the City of Mexico to the west, between the west and the north, and according to general belief, is between New Mexico and La Quivira, and if perhaps one should be mistaken, cosmography will help to record other kingdoms. One is called Chillescas, the other, the Kingdom of the Guismanes, and the other one, the Kingdom of the Aburcos, all of which border on this Kingdom of Tidam, and as soon as they are discovered, they will try to learn if in them, especially in El Tidam, there is word of our holy Catholic faith and through what medium and methods Our Lord has manifested it to them.

CXXXVII.

I, Archbishop Elect of Mexico, D. Francisco Manzo y Zúñiga,[1] of the Council of His Majesty and of the Real Council of the Indies, entreat the Reverend Fathers and Guardians of this conversion to make this inquiry, so that they will carry it out and request it with the promptness, faith, and devotion that such a case requires. And in order that, from what may result, they will have advised us in a way that we may know the truth. From this, without doubt will come great spiritual and temporal advancements to the honor and glory of God Our Lord. Given in Mexico on the 18th day of the month of May of 1682 [sic].

LICENCIADO FRANCISCO MANZO Y ZÚÑIGA.

CXXXVIII.

This is, Most Reverend Father, what has been seen, heard, and known, on sea as well as on land; and I certify to Your Reverence, that I have not thought it over with the earnestness that I could have, for I would rather appear stupid, resembling unbelieving men, who usually have not left their villages, nor do they know anyone except a priest and a sacristan. And thus everything that they hear seems impossible to them, and (they think) that the world is not as large as it is represented, because they can only understand what is within their range of vision. But to experienced and well read men, none of this confuses their understanding, since, as they possess it, they comprehend this and much more.

The truth is, that in not carrying out fully the exploration of this land, His Majesty loses a great world; and may our Lord guard your most reverend fatherhood as all of us, your children, desire. Amen. Laus Deo.

Footnotes

INTRODUCTION

1. These friars are mentioned in documents of 1626, A.G.N. Inquisición, tomo 356, ff. 257-316. France Vinton Scholes and Lansing B. Bloom, "Friar Personnel and Mission Chronology, 1598-1629," *New Mexico Historical Review,* Volume XX, 1945, p. 62.

2. For more information on this subject read France V. Scholes, "Church and State in New Mexico in the 17th Century," *New Mexico Historical Review,* Volume XI, 1936, University of New Mexico, Albuquerque.

3. France V. Scholes, "Church and State in New Mexico in the 17th Century," *NMHR,* Volume XI, p. 289.

4. Fray Esteban Perea was a great leader of the Church in New Mexico. For some 30 years after 1609 he was the dominant figure in its religious life. Henry R. Wagner, *The Spanish Southwest—1542-1794,* The Quivira Society, Volume VII, Albuquerque, New Mexico, 1937, p. 234.

5. Jack D. Forbes, *Apache, Navaho and Spaniard,* University of Oklahoma Press, Norman, Oklahoma, 1960, p. 114.

6. Hubert Howe Bancroft, *Arizona and New Mexico, History of the Pacific States of North America,* Volume XII, The History Company Publishers, San Francisco, California, 1888, pp. 21, 79, 159, 160.

7. France V. Scholes, "Documents for the History of the New Mexico Missions in the 17th Century," *New Mexico Historical Review, Volume* IV, 1929, pp. 45, 46. Title: Mexico, Ecclesiastical 1664, The Provincial of the Order of Saint Francis of the Province of the Santo Evangelio concerning the matter of granting 40 friars to the said province. Information may also be found in Inquisicion Papers in the Archivo General de la Nación, Mexico City.

8. Fray Francisco de Apodaca became commissary in 1627. He came from the Franciscan Province of Cantabria and returned to his native country in Spain in 1633. Francisco Antonio de la Rosa Figueroa, O.F.M., Bezerro General, Menológico y Chronólogico de Todos los Religiosos que Ha Avido en esta Sta. Prova. del Sto. Evango. desde su Fundación hasta el Presente Año de 1764. MS in Ayer Collection, Newberry Library, Chicago, p. 35.

9. José Tudela de la Orden, *Los Manuscritos de América en las Bibliotecas de España,* Ediciones Cultura Hispánica, Madrid, 1954, pp. 61, 62, 78, 287. Herbert E. Bolton, *Guide to Materials for the History of the United States in the Principal Archives of Mexico,* Washington D.C., 1913, pp. 20, 21, 22, 235.

APPROVAL

10. Fray Francisco de Apodaca, see note 8 of the introduction.

11. Fray Francisco de Velasco was a cousin of Oñate and joined his

colony at San Gabriel in December, 1600. He accompanied Oñate to the plains in 1601. He "was seemingly the Velasco who was 'lector jubilado' and provincial of the Holy Evangel of Mexico at best between August 1629 and July 1634." According to Vetancurt, Fray Francisco de Velasco was born in Tecamachalco, Mexico. Frederick Webb Hodge, George P. Hammond, Agapito Rey, *Fray Alonso de Benavides' Revised Memorial of 1634,* The University of New Mexico Press, Albuquerque, New Mexico, 1945, p. 203.

12. Mark 16:15
13. Matthew 10:28
14. Hemex is Jemez.
15. Zia.
16. Lamentations 4:4
17. Zechariah 4:6
18. Matthew 9:38
19. Psalms 91:15

THE NEWS BEGINS

I.

1. Antonio de Mendoza, nobleman born in Granada, Spain, at the end of the XV century, was the first Viceroy of New Spain from 1535-1550. He died in Lima, Peru, in 1552, having served there as Viceroy since 1550. He founded the University of Mexico and it is believed that he brought the first printing press to Mexico. He was one of the best viceroys. *Enciclopedia Universal Ilustrada Europeo-Americana,* Tomo XXXIV, Espasa Calpe, S.A., Bilbao, Madrid, Barcelona, España, p. 622.

2. New Spain is now Mexico.

3. Marqués del Valle de Oaxaca, D. Hernán Cortés de Monroy y Pizarro. José Ignacio Dávila Garibi, *Apuntes para la Historia de la Iglesia en Guadalajara,* Tomo I. Editorial Cultura, T.G.S.A., México, D.F. 1957.

4. Pacific Ocean.

5. Fray Antonio de Ciudad Rodrigo from the Franciscan Province of San Gabriel, was one of the first 12 Franciscans who came to New Spain, arriving in Vera Cruz on May 13, 1524. He was the founder of the Province of the Santo Evangelio and its second provincial. Charles the Fifth appointed him to be the first bishop of Nueva Galicia but he did not accept. He journeyed to Spain to petition on behalf of the Indians asking that those who had been sold as slaves be given their liberty. He died on September 13, 1553, and is buried in the Convent of San Francisco in Mexico City. Dávila Garibi, *Apuntes para la Historia de la Iglesia en Guadalajara,* Tomo I, pp. 269, 270, 394.

II.

1. Associated with the Coronado expedition were: Fray Pedro Nadal and Fray Juan de la Asunción, Pablo Martínez, Fray Marcos, and Fray Onorato, a lay brother who became ill on the way and returned. George P. Hammond and Agapito Rey, *Narratives of the Coronado Expedition,* Volume II; University of New Mexico Press, Albuquerque, New Mexico, 1946, p. 61.

2. Nueva Galicia now known as Sinaloa, Mexico.

III.

1. Matthew 11:25
2. Fray Marcos de Niza. Variously spelled Fray Marcos Denia.

IV.

1. Fray Marcos de Niza. Fray Juan de Padilla, zealous and fearless missionary, came from Andalucía, Spain, and was martyred in Kansas. Fray Juan de la Cruz was martyred in Bernalillo. (Said by some to be the monastic name for Fray Luis de Escalona.) See Bandelier's discussion of this point: *New Mexico Historical Review,* Vol. V, pp. 174-184). Fray Luis de Escalona, also called Luis de Ubeda, was martyred in Pecos. Fray Antonio Victoria broke his leg near Culiacán and stayed behind. Lucas and Sebastian, Indian lay brothers, returned to New Spain with the Portuguese, Andrés del Campo. Another friar is mentioned by Coronado on two different occasions, Fray Antonio de Castilblanco. Perhaps he is the same as Fray Antonio Victoria, George P. Hammond and Agapito Rey, *Narratives of the Coronado Expedition,* Volume II, University of New Mexico Press, Albuquerque, New Mexico, 1946, pp. 9-12, p. 307. In a letter dated August 3, 1540, addressed to Viceroy Mendoza, a Fray Daniel, an Italian, appears as a member of Coronado's band, *Historia Eclesiástica Indiana,* (Mendieta's History, 1596), Mexico, 1870, pp. 744-745.

V.

1. Really Hernando de Alarcón, born in Trujillo, Extremadura, Spain, in 1500; he left Acapulco, Mexico, in 1540, to take supplies for the Coronado Expedition and failed to meet. Herbert E. Bolton, *Coronado, Knight of Pueblos and Plains,* Whittlesey House, McGraw-Hill Company, Inc.; New York, London, Toronto, and The University of New Mexico Press, Albuquerque, New Mexico, 1949, pp. 103-107, p. 112.

VI.

1. Culiacán.
2. Valle de Corazones is near Ures, Sonora, Mexico, so called when the natives gave Dorantes 600 deer hearts because Cabeza de Vaca went through there. Herbert E. Bolton, *Coronado,* pp. 10-11.
3. Zuñi, Cibola.
4. This was the detachment under Melchior Díaz, great scout and be-

loved commander, who died after a tragic accident on his return journey from the Colorado River area. He is now sleeping in an unknown grave on the Camino del Diablo, between the Colorado River and Sonora Valley, Herbert E. Bolton, *Coronado* pp. 169-176, p. 380.

5. The head of the Gulf of California is actually in latitude 30° 50' north.

6. Morrillos—variously spelled Moros, natives of the Philippines.

7. "The name Quivira was first employed by the chroniclers of the Coronado Expedition in 1540-1542 to designate the Wichita and their tribal range in the present Kansas. (See Hammond and Rey, *Narratives of the Coronado Expedition;* Winship, *The Coronado Expedition*)." Frederick Webb Hodge, George P. Hammond, Agapito Rey, *Fray Alonso de Benavides' Revised Memorial of 1634,* The University of New Mexico Press, Albuquerque, New Mexico, 1945, p. 319.

8. Luke 14:20

VII.

1. Atlantic Ocean.

2. New France as used here refers to the Atlantic seaboard of North America in general and the Dutch in New York.

VIII.

1. For the route of return see Herbert E. Bolton, *Coronado.*

2. Indian lay brothers wearing the habit of friars.

3. Fray Agustín Ruiz known as Fray Agustín Rodríguez, native of Ayamonte del Condado, Spain, a lay brother, wearing the habit of Saint Francis, was the author and principal agent of this discovery. He obtained the grant and commission for the people who went on this expedition from D. Lorenzo Suárez de Mendoza, Count of Coruña, Viceroy and Captain-General of New Spain and President of the Audiencia and Royal Chancery. He asked for two friars to help him carry out and direct the expedition and to administer the sacraments. Fray Francisco López, a native of Sevilla, Spain, went as guardian. Fray Juan de Santa María, a native of Valencia, Spain, also went. Both of these priests were Franciscans. Captain Francisco Sánchez Chamuscado, a native of the bishopric of Coria, Cáceres, Extremadura, Spain, born in Arroyo del Puerto, took eight good soldiers along, these were men of great courage. This exploration was started on June 6, 1581. They explored the provinces of San Felipe, New Mexico, *Obregón's History of 16th Century Explorations in Western America,* entitled *Chronicle, Commentary, or Relation of the Ancient and Modern Discoveries in New Spain and New Mexico, Mexico, 1584.* Translated, edited and annotated by George P. Hammond, and Agapito Rey; Wetzel Publishing Company, Inc., Los Angeles, California, 1928, pp. 268-269.

4. Río del Norte was the Río Grande.

5. Zárate Salmerón uses the word "astrologer."

6. Puaray Mountains known as Sandía Mountains.

7. Macana, a rod half a vara long with a thick stone head attached.

8. Real, a silver coin worth about one-third of a peso.

X.

1. Antonio de Espejo was a native of the town of Torre Milano near Córdoba, Spain. He was the instrument and principal promoter in assembling this expedition, giving those who went with him everything that they needed. Espejo obtained his commission for the expedition from the authorities of Santa Barbola, at Cuatro Ciénegas, a settlement 70 leagues east of Santa Barbara. On November 10, 1582, Captain Antonio de Espejo with his soldiers left from San Bartolomé, which is under the jurisdiction of the town and mines of Santa Barbola. After marching two days, Fray Pedro de Heredia, who had left with the group from San Bartolomé, received instructions to return, and his duties were given to Fray Bernaldino Beltrán, who joined them at this place, along with other friars. The wife and children of one of the soldiers also went on this journey. Hammond and Rey, *Obregón's History,* pp. 316-317. See also Herbert E. Bolton, *Spanish Explorations in the Southwest,* pp. 168-169, for Espejo's account. The original manuscript bears an incorrect dating of 1538.

2. Espejo called New Mexico, Nueva Andalucía, in memory of his native province.

XI.

1. Gaspar Castaño de Sosa, Lieutenant Governor of Nuevo León and a frontier captain, led an unauthorized expedition into New Mexico in 1590. He was taken back and arrested by Juan Morlete, who had been sent by the Viceroy. Gaspar Castaño de Sosa left a good account. Zárate Salmerón's account has Nemorcete for Morlete.

2. In 1593, Captain Francisco Leyva de Bonilla led an illegal expedition into New Mexico for the purpose of acquiring quick wealth. They went on out to a great pueblo of the Vaqueros (Plains Apaches) on the plains in the midst of the multitude of buffalo. They were in search of Coronado's long lost Quivira. Shortly thereafter a soldier named Antonio Gutiérrez de Humaña murdered Captain Leyva and assumed command of the expedition. This probably took place along the Arkansas River among the Wichita group of Indians. They were later killed by the Wichita Indians. Jack D. Forbes, *Apache, Navaho and Spaniard,* University of Oklahoma Press; Norman, Oklahoma, 1960, pp. 75, 76.

3. "The exact date of Fray Esteban Perea's appointment is not known. . . . In Perea's statement he had been Superior Prelate of New Mexico three times. He was Commissary in 1614, Custodian from 1616-1617 to 1621 and Custodian from 1629 to 1631." The identification for the first period is based on Zárate

Salmerón's account. The identification for the second period comes from various sources. The third period is based on Perea's own account. For more detailed information read the works of France V. Scholes, "Church and State in New Mexico," *Publications in History*, Volume VII, June 1937, Historical Society of New Mexico, University of New Mexico Press, Albuquerque, June, 1937, p. 37.

XIII.

1. Puerto de Zalagua currently Manzanillo, Colima, Mexico.

2. The entrance to the Gulf of California between La Paz and Mazatlán is 211 miles wide. In other parts it is 120 miles wide.

XIV.

1. Romans 3:13

XV.

1. See earlier footnote, section 1, fn. 3.

XVII.

1. Quintos del Rey, the King's portion, traditionally a fifth.

XVIII.

1. Cape Mendocino is actually in latitude 40° 20′.

2. Zárate Salmerón credits the naming of Cape Mendocino to the Manila Galleon. Some doubt exists as to its being named after the Viceroy D. Antonio de Mendoza. Some are inclined to believe that it was named in honor of Lorenzo Suárez de Mendoza, Count of Coruña, Viceroy of New Spain from 1580 to 1582.

XIX.

1. Newfoundland.

2. The Strait of Anian was the mythical and imaginary strait which was sought by numerous European explorers, and is frequently correlated with the Northwest Passage. See Henry R. Wagner, *Spanish Voyages to the Northwest Coast of America in the 16th Century*, San Francisco, 1929.

XX.

1. Toribio Gómez de Corbán was an experienced admiral who was with Vizcaíno on several journeys, Alvaro del Portillo y Díez Sollano, *Descubrimientos y Exploraciones en las Costas de California*. Publicaciones de la Escuela de Estudios Hispano-Americanos de Sevilla, Madrid, 1947, p. 190.

2. Friars of the Carmelite Order.

3. Currently Cape Blanco.

4. Río Santiago.

5. Refers to Thomas Cavendish. According to some sources there is a possibility that Vizcaíno was not on the Manila Galleon in 1587.

6. Acaponeta.

7. Nayarit.

8. When there did not seem to be an English equivalent, I have kept the original Spanish. *Cornudas* are baby sharks one year old or under. Topes are small sharks, *Chuchos* are a fish of the ray family. Francisco J. Santamaría, *Diccionario General de Americanismos* (3 volumes).

XXII.

1. The *Santa Ana* was robbed at San Barnabé and not at this place. Vizcaíno was here looking for the *Santa Ana* in 1585.

2. Isla de Cenizas is the same as Isla de Cedros.

3. San Hipólito Bay is south of Cedros Island.

4. Russians. The word Muscovites is more accurate for the period.

5. These four islands were named Los Coronados on November 8, 1602, by the friars of the Vizcaíno Expedition because that day was the day of the Four Coronados, four brothers allegedly put to death for their Christian faith at the time of Diocletian.

6. Mission Bay.

7. Today Catalina Island. The Indians on this island were the Chumash.

8. Characteristic plank canoes of the Chumash Indians. A. L. Kroeber, *Handbook of the Indians of California,* California Book Company, Ltd., Berkeley, California, August 1953, by permission of the Chief of the Bureau of American Ethnology, Smithsonian Institution, p. 803.

9. Monterey, named after D. Gaspar de Zúñiga y Acevedo, Conde de Monterrey, Viceroy of New Spain from 1595 to 1603, at which time he was appointed Viceroy of Peru, where he died in 1606.

XXIV.

1. A *vara* is a variable unit of length about 2.8 feet. A span, or *jeme,* is the distance from the end of the thumb to the end of the forefinger (both extended). It is also given as 5.4772 inches in J. Villasana Haggard, *Handbook for Translators of Spanish Historical Documents,* Semco Press, p. 77.

2. This seems exaggerated.

3. *Palmo,* a measure of length (8.23 inches), J. Villasana Haggard, *Handbook for Translators of Spanish Historical Documents,* p. 81.

XXV.

1. Puerto de San Francisco is now Drake's Bay.

2. See Robert F. Heizer, "Archaeological Evidence of Sebastián Rodríguez Cermeño's Visit in 1595." *California Historical Society Quarterly,* December 1941, pp. 315-328.

XXVI.

1. 43 degrees should have brought them in sight of the Rogue River.

XXVII.

1. As a result of this reasoning there appeared a shift in location of Quivira to Oregon.

XXVIII.

1. The Conde de Monterrey was made Viceroy of Peru in 1603.

XXIX.

1. By Pilot Morea. See Section CXVIII.

2. Newfoundland.

3. The imaginary Strait of Anian, and the mythical tales of 16th century explorers.

4. San Juan de Ulúa is part of the harbor of Vera Cruz.

5. Rodrigo del Río de Losa came as a soldier in 1563 to serve on the northern frontier of Chihuahua and Sonora, fighting the Indians who were revolting. He took an active part in explorations and was an outstanding soldier. He was important in Nuevo León and Texas.

XXXIII.

1. See George P. Hammond, *Don Juan de Oñate and the Founding of New Mexico,* Santa Fe, New Mexico, 1927. See also George P. Hammond and Agapito Rey, *Don Juan de Oñate, Colonizer of New Mexico, 1595-1628,* University of New Mexico Press, Albuquerque, New Mexico, 1953. See Herbert E. Bolton, *Spanish Explorations in the Southwest, 1542-1706,* Scribners, New York, 1916.

XXXIV.

1. Visita, an official military inspection.

2. Río del Norte is the Río Grande.

3. Río del Zama is the Río Chama.

4. Site of San Gabriel (de los Españoles), first European town in the west and second in the United States of America.

5. Orantes is Andrés Dorantes.

6. Saint Lawrence River.

7. Mina here refers to mining camp sites which have not been worked.

8. "Puaray." The Sandía Mountains.

9. "Siénega." Ciénega is a marsh or a moor in Spanish.

10. Hemex is Jemez.

11. One arroba is a little more than 25 pounds.

XXXV.

1. D. Pedro de Peralta was governor of New Mexico from 1610 to 1614.

XXXVI.

1. Bagres, catfish.

2. Matalote, a river fish.

3. Adelantado, a frontier captain armed with extensive civil and military authority.

XXXVII.

1. Antonio Gutiérrez de Humaña. See note 2, Section XI.

2. Vaqueros are the Apaches.

XXXVIII.

1. Escansaques Indians [also Escanxaques] are the Kansas Indians. Escansaques variously spelled throughout the text.

2. There is no other evidence that Humaña found any gold.

3. Ahijados, Ayjados, Aijados, Aixaos, variously spelled throughout the text. "The Aixaos Indians were placed 30 or 40 leagues east of Quivira or in southern Oklahoma (according to Benavides). The Aixos mentioned by Benavides were evidently not the inhabitants of the province called 'Harahey' by Jaramillo, and 'Harle' by the *Relación del Suceso* (see Winship, *Coronado;* and Hammond and Rey, *Narratives of the Coronado Expedition*), which adjoined the Quivira Province in 1541 and which we have identified with the Pawnee country; but more likely the 'Haxa,' who, while on the Texas plains, Coronado learned were farther east from where his army then was." "The present writer is inclined to think that the Aixos (or Haxas) were the Eyeish (Aix, Ayas, Ay, etc.), a tribe of the Caddo Confederacy which lived in eastern Texas, and was gathered in the Mission of Nuestra Señora de los Ais, near the Sabine River, in 1716." Frederick Webb Hodge, George P. Hammond, Agapito Rey, *Fray Alonso de Benavides' Revised Memorial of 1634,* p. 319. "Coronado in 1540-41 learned of a settlement called Ayas at which the Spanish army could obtain provisions," Frederick Webb Hodge, *Handbook of American Indians North of Mexico,* Part 1, pp. 448-449.

XLIV.

1. "Iztli" variation in spelling of ixtle. Ixtle, Aztec generic name for all kinds of vegetable fibers and also given to the fiber of the agaves and the plants belonging to it and which form fiber. Ixtle de Jaumave is one of the agaves which produces the finest fiber in Mexico and is peculiar to the northern part of the country. It is also cultivated in Europe. Francisco J. Santamaría, *Diccionario General de Americanismos.*

2. Moqui or sometimes Mogui or Mooqui—the Hopi Indians, speaking a Shoshonean dialect in northeastern Arizona, Frederick Webb Hodge, *Handbook of American Indians North of Mexico,* Part I, p. 560.

XLV.

1. The first Zuñi pueblo was Hawikuh. Jack D. Forbes, *Apache, Navaho, and Spaniard,* University of Oklahoma Press: Norman, Oklahoma, 1960.

2. Homex: Jemez.

XLVI.

1. This is the Little Colorado River. Jack D. Forbes, *Apache, Navaho and Spaniard*, p. 105.

2. The Cruzado Indians have always been identified as the early Yavapai. Jack D. Forbes, *Apache, Navaho, and Spaniard*, p. 61. In 1583, in the area of present-day Jerome, Arizona, the Spaniards found these Cruzado Indians, even the children, wearing crosses made of reeds on their foreheads and dressed in buckskin garments. This was the Flagstaff-Jerome region. Jack D. Forbes, *Apache, Navaho, and Spaniard*, pp. 86, 93, 104.

XLVII.

1. "Amacava": Mojave Indians. Jack D. Forbes, *Apache, Navaho, and Spaniard*, p. 104.

2. Pitaya, pitahaya, the cereus giganteus whose fruit was much used as food by the tribes of the Southwest. See Bolton's *Spanish Explorations*, p. 271.

3. Río de Buena Esperanza is the Colorado River. Río del Tizón, (River of the Firebrands), is a continuation of the Colorado River near the sea, and is called thus because the Indians of this Yuma area, when they traveled about from place to place, carried a firebrand with which they warmed their hands and body, changing it from one hand to the other from time to time as they traveled along. In cold weather the firebrand was their blanket which they threw away when the sun got warm and there were so many of them cast along the roads that they would serve as a guide for travelers. Herbert E. Bolton, *Coronado*, p. 171.

4. The Duero River, famous in Spain's historical past, crosses through Castilla la Vieja and on into Portugal and the Atlantic. The Duero flows through Soria where Agreda is situated. This latter place was where María Jesús de Agreda lived when she appeared to the Jumano Indians in the New Mexico region. Her last visit was made in 1691. She converted these tribes "in ecstasy." The story of the Lady in Blue is now a classic in the lore of the Southwest. John Francis Bannon, *Bolton, and the Spanish Borderlands*, University of Oklahoma Press: Norman, Oklahoma, 1964, pp. 104-105.

5. The Guadalquivar River which flows through Sevilla in Andalucía, is the second most important river in Spain and the only navigable one. It is famous in song and history.

XLVIII.

1. Late in 1603 or early in 1604, a party of Spaniards led by Captain Gerónimo Márquez visited Acoma, Zuñi, and the Hopi pueblos. From the Hopi pueblos the group made its way to the lands of the Cruzados and the mines near Jerome. Jack D. Forbes, *Apache, Navaho, and Spaniard*, p. 103.

XLIX.

1. Laguna de Copalla in Mexican myth doubtless later refers to Lake Chapala in the eastern part of the state of Jalisco, Mexico, and to Santa Barbara, in southern Chihuahua. "These . . . Indians traveled more than 400 leagues from Lago Copala where they had first settled to the valley which we now call Santa Barbara." Frederick Webb Hodge, George P. Hammond, Agapito Rey, *Fray Alonso de Benavides' Revised Memorial of 1634,* The University of New Mexico Press, Albuquerque, New Mexico, 1945, pp. 41, 231.

2. At the time of the Viceroy D. Luis de Velasco (1550-?) and when the earliest explorations were made, the early name of New Mexico was Copalla, Hammond and Rey, *Obregon's History,* pp. 43, 50.

L.

1. Amacabos, a variant spelling for Mojaves. These are the Hamakhava. A. L. Kroeber, *Handbook of the Indians of California,* p. 727. See Frederick Webb Hodge, *Handbook of American Indians North of Mexico,* Government Printing Office, Washington, 1910.

LII.

1. Río del Nombre de Jesús is the Gila River.

2. The legend of La Giganta ties in with the Amazon legend. "The mythical island, Zinogaba, in the sea sounds as if it might be named from a woman, *thenya'aka* in Mohave, and ava, house. Its chieftainess, Cinaca cohota, is certainly "woman-kohota." The native information now accumulated allows the valuable findings of the Oñate expedition of 1605, as related by Zárate Salmerón, to be profitably summarized, reinterpreted, and compared with those of later date." A. L. Kroeber, *Handbook of the Indians of California,* pp. 803, 802.

LIII.

1. "Halchedoma": variously spelled Halchidoma. The Halchidoma is a group of Indians on the Colorado River. A. L. Kroeber, *Handbook of the Indians of California,* p. 801.

2. Cocopas variously spelled Cocopahs.

LV.

1. "Most colonial territories were claimed or acquired by the symbolical ritual of taking possession. It was a religious ceremony as well as a legal act. The conversion of the heathen continued to be the basis for acquisition of American lands by European powers. The honor of beginning the occupation movement in North America, as represented by the performance of acts of possession, justly belongs to the intrepid explorers and navigators of the Hispanic peninsula." "The ceremony of taking possession definitely became more religious. Juan de Oñate's act of 1598 in New Mexico vividly typifies such a

characteristic as it sounds more like a prayer than a religious document. Oñate states the basis upon which possession is taken . . . . the conversion of the heathen . . . . and strongly bases the Spanish claim upon the donation of Pope Alexander VI. ('As a sign of true and pacific possession . . . . he placed and nailed the Holy Cross of Our Redeemer Jesus Christ and . . . . he said: "Cross you are holy . . . . open Heaven's door to these infidels.').'' Manuel Servín, "Religious Aspects of Symbolic Acts of Sovereignty," *The Americas,* Volume XIII, January 1957, Academy of American Franciscan History, Washington, D.C., p. 259.

LVI.

1. The Spaniards called this valley Señora. This word was a corruption of the native name of Sonora, which today is applied to the river, to the valley, and to the large state in northwestern Mexico. In the place name Opata has prevailed over Castilian. Herbert E. Bolton, *Coronado,* p. 151.

LVIII.

1. John Davis, English navigator born in Sandridge, Devonshire about 1550 and died December 30, 1605. In 1585 he was sent out with two vessels to find a northwest passage when he discovered the strait which still bears his name.

LIX.

1. Henry Hudson was English; he was sailing for the Dutch.

LXII.

1. Expectations that they would find these mythological monsters caused them to report their existence.

2. Sebastián Gavoto known as Sebastian Cabot was a Venetian born in 1474 and died in London in 1557. There is some doubt as to his place and date of birth, some believing that he was born in Bristol, England. *Enciclopedia Universal Ilustrada Europea-Americana,* tomo X, Espasa Calpe, p. 10.

LXIV.

1. Cabo de Bacallaos is known as Cape Cod.

2. Atlantic Ocean and Pacific Ocean. The strait refers to the mythological Strait of Anian, also called the Northwest Passage.

3. "Cortes Reales": Named after Gaspar Corte Real, one of two Portuguese brothers who explored this coast in 1500.

LXIX.

1. Río de las Damas.

LXXIII.

1. Chicoria, Chicora—variously spelled throughout the text. Chicora and

Orista were provinces on the Georgia coast that Lucas Vásquez de Ayllón discovered and explored in 1520. He named this place Santa Elena on account of having discovered it on the day of Santa Elena. Ayllón was looking for Utopia in Chicora, land of the giant King Datha. The story says "King Datha was not naturally monstrous, but in his childhood was merely rubbed with the juice of herbs and he stretched." Herbert E. Bolton, *Coronado*, p. 8.

LXXV.

1. Hernando Boyano, not Moyano, early explorer of the back country of Carolina and Georgia, brought back stories of wealth and treasure that circulated on the frontier for a century, grew bigger with each generation and inspired more than one expedition. "Tales of Spanish mines lured the English as well as the Spaniards. The Diamond Mountain tale and fear of foreign intrusion were intertwined with an ever recurrent desire to seek the pearls of Cufitachiqui or Boyano's Diamond Mountain." "Old tales of Boyano's Mountain were revived and stirred up new dreams of conquest in 1595. Spanish Expeditions were sent to investigate these rumors." Herbert E. Bolton, *Arrendondo's Historical Proof of Spain's Title to Georgia*, University of California Press, Berkeley, California, 1925, pp. 10, 16, 24.

LXXIX.

1. Cape Cañaveral is now Cape John F. Kennedy.

2. Guale is the old Spanish name for Georgia; the Georgia coast constituted the district of Guale but was specifically applied to Santa Catalina Island where the great Adelantado Menéndez de Aviles landed in April, 1566. The chief of this island was an old man named Guale. The name was gradually extended down the entire Georgia coast and was part of the province of Florida. Herbert E. Bolton, *Arredondo's Historical Proof of Spain's Title to Georgia*, pp. 8, 9.

3. Named in honor of Fray Alonso Reynoso, "devout, gentle, zealous, tireless, though shadowy in the distance, still looms large and strong. He was a 16th century Serra on the Atlantic coast, a hero of this early Franciscan period." Herbert E. Bolton, *Arredondo's Historical Proof of Spain's Title to Georgia*, p. 14.

4. Governor Pedro Menéndez Márquez, nephew of the Adelantado, Pedro Menéndez de Aviles, executed Nicolas Estrozi, head of one of the marauding bands of French corsairs, and 22 of his men at San Agustín in 1579. Herbert E. Bolton, *Arredondo's Historical Proof of Spain's Title to Georgia*, p. 13.

5. It was not Márquez who killed all the French except the women and children in the battle at Charlesfort, September 1565, but his uncle, Pedro Menéndez de Aviles, Governor and founder of San Agustín, Florida, Don Iñigo Abad y Lasierra, "Año de 1785, La Florida y La Luisiana, Siglos XVI al

XVIII, Relacion del Descubrimiento," *Conquista* y Población de las Provincias *y Costas de la Florida,* Librería General de Victoriano Suárez, Madrid, 1912, pp. 68, 69.

6. "Juan de Ribao": Jean Ribaut founded the ill-starred French colony of Port Royal which failed in 1562. Herbert E. Bolton, *Arredondo's Historical Proof of Spain's Title to Georgia,* p. 7.

LXXX.

1. Luis Moscoso was second in command to Hernando de Soto, who upon dying appointed Moscoso leader of the expedition. Herbert E. Bolton, *Coronado,* p. 355.

2. See Herbert E. Bolton, *Coronado,* for details of Hernando de Soto's Expedition, pp. 15, 40-45, 275-281, 290, 303-304, 355-356.

LXXXI.

1. Spelled Iribaracusi in Section LXXX.

XCII.

1. Acuse.

2. Mobile.

3. An *estado* is two varas, 1.83 yard. J. Villasana Haggard, *Handbook for Translators of Spanish Historical Documents,* p. 761.

XCIII.

1. "Chicaza": Chickasaw.

2. Alibamo, currently Alabama. Vara, refer back to note 1, Section XXIV. Guadalquivir, refer back to note 5, Section XLVII.

3. Orantes is Dorantes, member of Cabaza de Vaca's group.

XCVIII.

1. Río Grande here refers to the Mississippi River.

2. Virginia, named in honor of Queen Elizabeth.

C.

1. Panuco is Tampico.

CII.

1. Colorado River.

2. Sonora.

3. Río Grande.

4. Chama.

CIII.

1. Nahuatl, the language of the Aztecs.

CIV.

1. "Azapuzalco": Azcapotzalco, suburb of modern Mexico City.

2. The west coast route to Mexico from Utah.

CV.

1. For story of this iron formation, see Gaspar Pérez de Villagra, *History of New Mexico,* Alcalá, 1616, pp. 46, 47, 48, 49.

CVI.

1. Quintal, 100 pounds.

2. "A demon in the guise of an old woman carried an enormous and terrible boulder of iron on her head." For the story of this huge boulder see Frederick Webb Hodge, George P. Hammond, Agapito Rey, *Fray Alonso de Benavides' Revised Memorial of 1634,* pp. 40, 41.

CIX.

1. Fray Francisco de Velasco, refer to note 11, Approval.

2. Captain Vicente de Zaldívar Mendoza, nephew of Oñate, went with him in 1601 and led an expedition into the plains of the buffalo country. Herbert E. Bolton, *Spanish Explorations in the Southwest, 1542-1706,* pp. 223, 231, 251, 268.

CXIII.

1. This is the first known historical reference to the Navajos. While Zárate Salmerón was at Jemez, before 1623, he became acquainted with the Navajo Apaches who told him that beyond their nation there was a large river that flowed into the Lagoon of Copalla. They spoke of the Quiajules who were also Navajos, and of the Utes. Jack D. Forbes, *Apache, Navaho and Spaniard,* p. 115. (From Zárate Salmerón, *Virreinato de Méjico,* tomo I, Museo Naval 567.)

2. Río Colorado.

3. The Qusutas were the Utes. Charles Amsden, "Navajo Origins," *New Mexico Historical Review,* Volume VII, no. 3, July 1932, pp. 199, 200.

CXV.

1. Río Grande.

2. The Cojoyas were Opatas.

3. "In the El Paso area lived the Mansos, called by Zárate Salmerón the Gorretas (Little Caps) because of their hair style, which was trimmed to look as if they were wearing caps. The Opatas, their western neighbors, were called Cojoias by Zárate Salmerón—both these tribes came to see the Spaniards. In 1621 a group of new priests arrived in New Mexico and among them was Fray Gerónimo de Zárate Salmerón, our chief source of information on New Mexico for the following five years." Jack D. Forbes, *Apache, Navaho, and Spaniard,* pp. 114, 116. Zárate Salmerón, *Virreinato de Méjico,* tomo I, MN 567.

4. Hot Springs, almost in Colorado.

5. "Tepeguanes": Tepehuanes.

CXIX.

1. N. de Morera possibly means that they did not know what his first name was and they used N. as the equivalent of Mr. X. Martín Fernández de Navarrete, *Colección de Documentos Inéditos para la Historia de España,* Volume 15, Impr. de la Viuda de Calero, Madrid, 1842.

2. Francis Drake.

CXX.

1. He traveled from California to New Mexico.

2. A patache is a skiff.

CXXII.

1. Mar Rojo, sometimes called Mar Bermejo or Mar de Cortés; on the American atlas it is the Gulf of California.

CXXIII.

1. Acts 1:7. It is not for you to know the time or the seasons, which the Father hath in his own power.

CXXVI.

1. Quauhuecholan, a fertile place not far from Puebla, Mexico, Fray Agustín de Vetancurt, *Teatro Mexicano, Crónica de la Provincia del Santo Evangelio de México,* Cuarta Parte, Tomo III, Imprenta de I. Escalante y Ca., Mexico, 1871, pp. 224-225.

2. Blessed are the first.

CXXIX.

1. Río Grande.

CXXXV.

1. Terranova, currently Newfoundland.

CXXXVII.

1. Francisco Manzo de Zúñiga, Archbishop of Mexico from 1629 to 1635. He was born in Cañas, Spain. In 1629 there were great inundations in Mexico City and Archbishop Manzo de Zúñiga performed outstanding rescue work going out personally in a canoe to take food to the victims. He was concerned with the welfare of the Indians. Fr. Agustín de Vetancurt, *Teatro Mexicano,* Tomo II, p. 290.

Bibliography

Abad y Lasserra, Don Iñigo. "Año de 1785, La Florida y La Luisiana, Siglos VI al XVIII, Relación del Descubrimiento," *Conquista y Pobalación de las Provincias y Costas de la Florida*. Libería General de Victoriano Suárez: Madrid, España. 1912.

Amsden, Charles. "Navajo Origins," *New Mexico Historical Review*, Volume VII, No. 3. The University of New Mexico Press: Albuquerque, New Mexico, 1932.

Ayer Collection, Newberry Library. Chicago, Illinois.

Bancroft, Hubert Howe. *Arizona and New Mexico, History of the Pacific States of North America*. The History Company Publishers: San Francisco, California. 1888.

Bandelier, Adolph F. A. "Documentary History of the Rio Grande Pueblos, New Mexico, Part I. 1536-1542." *New Mexico Historical Review*, Volume V. April 30, 1930.

Bannon, John Francis. *Bolton and the Spanish Borderlands*. University of Oklahoma Press: Norman, Oklahoma. 1964.

Bolton, Herbert E. *Arredondo's Historical Proof of Spain's Title to Georgia*. University of California Press: Berkeley, California. 1925.

————. *Coronado, Knight of Pueblos and Plains*. Whittlesey House: New York. 1949.

————. *Guide to Materials for the History of the United States in the Principal Archives of Mexico*. Carnegie Institution of Washington: Washington, D.C., 1913.

————. *Spanish Explorations in the Southwest, 1542-1706*. Scribners: New York. 1916.

Enciclopedia Universal Illustrada Europeo-Americana. Tomo X, Espasa Calpe, S. A.; Bilbao, Madrid, Barcelona; Espana. 1907-1930.

Fernández de Navarrete, Martín. *Colección de Documentos Inéditos para la Historia de España*, Volume 15. Imprenta de la Viuda de Calero: Madrid, Espana. 1842.

Forbes, Jack D. *Apache, Navaho, and Spaniard*. University of Oklahoma Press: Norman, Oklahoma. 1960.

Garibi, José Ignacio Davila. *Apuntes para la Historia de la Iglesia en Guadalajara*, Tomo I, Editorial Cultura, T.G.S.A.: Mexico D.F. 1957.

Haggard, J. Villasana. *Handbook for Translators of Spanish Historical Documents*. Semco Press:

Hammond, George P. *Don Juan de Oñate and the Founding of New Mexico.* El Palacio Press: Santa Fe, New Mexico. 1927.

———; Rey, Agapito. *Don Juan de Oñate, Colonizer of New Mexico, 1595-1628.* The University of New Mexico Press: Albuquerque, New Mexico. 1953.

———; ———. *Narratives of the Coronado Expedition,* Volume II. University of New Mexico Press: Albuquerque, New Mexico. 1946.

———; ———. (tr., ed.). *Obregon's History of 16th Century Explorations in Western America,* entitled, *Chronicle, Commentary, or Relation of the Ancient and Modern Discoveries in New Spain and New Mexico, Mexico, 1584.* Wetzel Publishing Company: Los Angeles. 1928.

Heizer, Robert F. "Archaeological Evidence of Sebastián Rodríguez Cermeño's Visit in 1595," *California Historical Society Quarterly,* December. 1941.

Historia Eclesiástica Indiana (Mendieta's History, 1596). Mexico. 1870.

Hodge, Frederick Webb. *Handbook of American Indians North of Mexico.* Government Printing Office: Washington, D.C. 1910.

———; Hammond, George P.; Rey, Agapito. *Fray Alonso de Benavides' Revised Memorial of 1634.* The University of New Mexico Press: Albuquerque, New Mexico. 1945.

Kroeber, A. L. *Handbook of the Indians of California.* California Book Company, Ltd.: Berkeley, California. 1953.

Pérez de Villagrá, Gaspar. See de Villagrá, Gaspar Pérez.

del Portillo, Alvaro; Sollano, Díez. *Descubrimientos y Exploraciones en las Costas de California.* Publicaciones de la Escuela de Estudios Hispano-Americanos de Sevilla: Madrid. 1947.

Santamaría, Francisco J. *Diccionario General de Americanismos,* III volumes. Editorial P. Robredo: Mexico D.F. 1942.

Scholes, France Vinton. "Church and State in New Mexico," *Publications in History,* Volume VII. The University of New Mexico Press: Albuquerque, New Mexico. 1937.

———. "Church and State in New Mexico in the 17th Century," *New Mexico Historical Review,* Volume XI. 1936.

———. "Documents for the History of the New Mexico Mission in the 17th Century," *New Mexico Historical Review,* Volume IV. 1929.

———; Bloom, Lansing B. "Friar Personnel and Mission Chronology, 1598-1629," *New Mexico Historical Review,* Volume XX. 1945.

Servín, Manuel. "Religious Aspects of Symbolic Acts of Sovereignty," *The Americas,* Volume XIII, January. Academy of American Franciscan History; Washington, D.C. 1957.

Tudela de la Orden, José. *Los Manuscritos de América en las Bibliotecas de España*. Ediciones Cultura Hispánica: Madrid. 1954.

de Vetancurt, Fray Agustín. *Teatro Mexicano, Crónica de la Provincia del Santo Evangelio de México*, Cuarta Parte, Tomo III. Imprenta de I. Escalante y Ca: México. 1871.

de Villagrá, Gaspar Pérez. *History of New Mexico*. Luys Martínez Grande: Alcala. 1610.

Wagner, Henry R. "The Spanish Southwest—1542-1794," *The Quivira Society*, Volume VII. Albuquerque, New Mexico. 1937.

————. *Spanish Voyages to the Northwest Coast of America in the 16th Century*. California Historical Society: San Francisco, California. 1929.

Winship, George Parker. *The Coronado Expedition 1540-1542*. Smithsonian Institution: Washington, D.C. 1896.

*The Publishers wish to thank Alicia Ronstadt
Milich for her painstaking research and study
which lead to the translation of Relaciones.
We wish also to thank Dr. Donald C.
Cutter for writing the foreword and assisting Mrs. Milich. We are excep-
tionally pleased with the title page,
jacket, and cover which were
designed by Arthur Lites.*